Another Epic Feat of Navigation Safely Completed!

by

Captain Jeremy Walker,
Master Mariner

Another Epic Feat of Navigation Safely Completed!

Jeremy Walker

ISBN: 978-1-7391206-0-3

Published by Welton Marine Publishing in conjunction with Writersworld. This book is produced entirely in the UK, is available to order from most book shops in the United Kingdom and is globally available via UK-based Internet book retailers and www.amazon.com.

Copy Edited by Ian Large

Cover Design by Jag Lall (www.jaglallart.com)

www.writersworld.co.uk

WRITERSWORLD

2 Bear Close Flats, Bear Close, Woodstock,
Oxfordshire, OX20 1JX, United Kingdom

☎ 01993 812500
☎ +44 1993 812500

The text pages of this book are produced via an independent certification process that ensures the trees from which the paper is produced come from well managed sources that exclude the risk of using illegally logged timber while leaving options to use post-consumer recycled paper as well.

Contents

Acknowledgements

Where do I start? There have been so many people who have helped and suffered my hours spent writing and talking about this book that I literally would need many pages to include them all.

Firstly, I must pay tribute to my long-suffering wife, Christine, who has supported me throughout and encouraged me to continue to labour away, to the detriment of all other household jobs that I should have been doing.

I cannot go any further without thanking my son-in-law Ash who, having listened to me regaling and telling some of these stories to his children (my grandchildren), said to me that I should write them all down as otherwise they would be lost. Without his suggestion, this book would not have been born.

I have to thank all my work colleagues over the 55 years of my career at or connected to the sea – my shipmates in Blue Funnel and Glen Lines, my 'hovering' friends in SeaSpeed, and not least my Piloting friends and associates in the Humber Pilot Service, who have provided me with the raw 'meat' for many of these tales. And then there were my fellow officers and the crew of the *Waverley* and the *New Advance* who taught me how to work again after losing the job I loved on the Humber.

To all my friends who have helped me to proofread and suffered me also telling them the ins and outs of a way of life that has now gone, they are numerous, and I mention just a few here with grateful thanks.

My oldest friend David Chambers and his wife, who have read all the stories and wallowed in memories of the past life that Dave and I shared all those years ago.

Rob Drewery, a village friend who also read and criticised each story, and my dear friend Kay Wilkinson, who also did the same and offered advice, suggestions and support during the long process.

My own son Alastair and daughter Hannah – the 'Caulk Heads' (as people born on the Isle of Wight are known) mentioned in 'Island Characters' – who helped with the technical side of the presentation.

But the final dedication must go to my late friend and colleague Robert Newton. 'Bob' would climb off a ship after completing an act of Pilotage on the River Humber and, with a wry smile on his face, utter his favourite catchphrase:

"Another Epic Feat of Navigation Safely Completed!"

Thank you, Bob, for the title of this book.

Another Epic Feat of Navigation Safely Completed!

As I sat on the side of Hamnafield on Foula in the Shetland Islands, looking down at my 'enormous' 38-foot ferry stowed in its cradle on the quay in Ham Voe, over 1000 feet below me, I reflected on a moderately successful career to date, and wondered how on Earth I had ended up driving what was, in effect, a floating dust cart.

Ham Voe from the peak of Hamnafield.

After 42 years at or connected with the sea, Jeremy Walker ended up on the Shetland Island of Foula commanding and running a small ferry to the mainland of Shetland. Throughout the course of his career, firstly as a seagoing Deck Officer with a large, but now defunct, British shipping company, then as a

Hovercraft Commander for four years, returning to sea for a brief period as Master of two small coastal tankers and then for the majority of his career as a Pilot on the River Humber, he encountered many amusing situations.

Floating dust cart.

In this book he attempts to relate these stories and to illustrate the lighter side of what was a very difficult, responsible and, at times, incredibly stressful job. And little did he know that his career was far from over and new opportunities and challenges would take him on for a further 13 years to eventual retirement.

Hell Pilot, You Might Have Told Me!

I suppose I couldn't really blame Captain Duncan Forester, but to a Pilot, a ship is a ship, is a ship, and the fact that it has a blue funnel makes no difference.

It had all started a few days earlier in July 1981. I had piloted a small container ship inward bound to King George Dock in Hull, and as I swung her off the jetty in the river to await entering the lock, there she was in plain view – the *Patroclus* – on 7 and 8 Shed, opposite the lock, lying in absolute splendour in her Blue Funnel colours – colours she had adopted since her transfer from Glen Line after her initial career as the *Glenalmond*. And my mind went back to those days, not too long before, when, as Second Officer on the *Glenfinlas* in 1969 and 1970 with the redoubtable Captain George Powell as Master, I had served out my time with Ocean Fleets. The eight ships built by Alfred Holt and Company (Ocean Fleets) as the Priam- and Glenalmond-class were the last to be built on conventional lines before the advent of containerisation, and they were splendid examples of British design and ingenuity. Powerful, fast, seaworthy ships that could carry anything from frozen prawns via general cargo and liquids in bulk, to individual pieces of cargo weighing up to 50 tons thanks to their heavy lift derricks.

And immediately one gets a yearning to have a go at piloting a 'real ship' once again.

As luck would have it, two evenings later the phone tinkled, summoning me to work. And there it was – the realisation of a dream since becoming a Pilot in 1975: "Job for you Jeremy, the *Patroclus*; 7/8 Shed, King George Dock to Sea; 1930 on board; you'll be sailing after the ferries probably…" and the Duty Pilot at Spurn probably rattled on for a bit longer but I didn't really hear him, I was too elated for words. I had sailed on this class of ship at the end of my career with Alfred Holt and Company, and prior to that on the *Flintshire*, one of the Glenlyon-class (predecessors of the Priams and Glenalmonds) and I had always admired the sheer power and grace of these ships, something that a Pilot appreciates more than anything else when he is forever handling Greek heaps with "…only enough air left for one more engine start, Mr Pilot…"

Still on cloud nine, I hastened to the dock and climbed aboard. The Midshipman, or should I say Midshipwoman/person/lady, who met me at the head of the gangway started off at a brisk pace towards the accommodation, determined to leave this silly sod of a Pilot behind her on the stairs. The trouble was she took the wrong ladder, which actually led to nowhere except the one deck above, and I had to say that I thought it better if we went this way, at which she looked decidedly flustered, then blushed, and agreed that it would. It's amazing how, when you serve on a ship for a while, you never forget your way about, no matter how long it has been since you were last on board. We arrived at the Captain's cabin, where I was introduced to Captain Duncan Forester, who I had sailed with many years previously when he was second mate on the *Antilochus* and we were 'coasting' her. (When a ship arrives back from Far Eastern ports, she visits many UK and Continental ports to discharge her cargo and load exports for the Far East again. A relief crew take her round these 'coastal' ports, giving the 'deep sea' crew a break, hence 'coasting' and 'deep sea' crews.)

Of course, he didn't remember me, I was only a lowly Fourth Mate and lasting friendships are not forged between Liverpool, Glasgow, Dublin and Birkenhead, particularly when everyone else has their wives with them and you are the only single bloke on board. The usual pre-departure kerfuffle was in full swing, and the Chief Officer was there, as well as the Agent, Cargo Superintendent, Marine Superintendent etc., and I was only so much superfluous baggage until they needed me. So I made my excuses to Captain Forester and escaped to the wheelhouse to call the dock and get the tugs organised – much more peaceful up there! It was where I had spent most of my time at sea as a Deck Officer on the various ships I had sailed on, keeping a bridge watch and navigating the ships between the many ports around the world I had visited while serving with Blue Funnel and Glen Lines. It contained all the navigation equipment, charts, radars, chronometers, radio direction-finding equipment and of course the wheel for steering as well as the automatic pilot and the engine room telegraph for issuing engine orders to the engineers down below in the main engine control room. It was the hub and nerve centre of any ship, vitally important to its safe passage across the oceans and it was a haven of peace after the hustle and bustle of the Captain's cabin where there were last minute decisions being made, which had nothing to do with me!

Entering the wheelhouse was like stepping back in time, a nostalgia trip that brought memories flooding back, and I felt at home. The Third Officer was a charming West African chap with whom I chatted over a cup of coffee, which he had immediately offered me on my entry to the bridge, and it was he who made it clear to me that this was the 'coasting' crew on board who had just joined the ship, and they were all finding their way around.

Eventually, Captain Forester appeared on the bridge and we shook hands once more. He had all the time in the world for me now that he had got rid of the shore bods, and we could get down to the nitty gritty of getting his ship out to sea. He asked me if I was familiar with the ship and I simply replied that I was, and it was left at that. I think one of the tugs called me on the radio at that moment to tell me he was made fast and that neatly sidestepped any further inquiries from Captain Forester. We left the berth in a calm and measured way, as was my style – locks don't go anywhere and they are always there two minutes later – all this spectacular manoeuvring with lots of 'full ahead' and 'full astern' looks great but if it goes wrong then it is equally spectacular; stones from the dock walls flying around in all directions is not a pretty sight!

I think I only used the engines half a dozen times in the dock, but I could feel that superb smooth power of the Sulzer 9RD90, 19,000 horse power main engine under my feet and the instant response to the rudder, so characteristic of the Priam- and Glenalmond-class. I had already had a word with the tugs to say that if I didn't like it when we approached the lock, I would put the immensely powerful ship's engines astern and could quite easily drag the head tug backwards out of the lock if necessary. The Hull tug Skippers are superb, but they can get carried away sometimes and a friendly word keeps them on their toes...

We settled in the lock quite happily and awaited the outer gates to open. More coffee was forthcoming – what a difference from the average Panamanian or Dutchman where you have to threaten murder for a glass of water! Then we were out in the river, that difficult turn outside the dock in the tideway to get her head to tide completed with such ease that is only experienced with a superbly designed ship that handles like a dream. Tugs dismissed, and then the 'faux pas'.

It was getting dark, a quarter to nine on a July evening, the light is starting to dwindle and the wheelhouse deckhead lights were still on. I politely asked Duncan Forester if they could be extinguished and I stood amused for ½ minute or so as I watched the Captain, Third Mate and Midshipperson hunting round on the bridge, around all the door frames, light fittings; everywhere except the correct place for the switch to turn off the lights. I could resist no longer and reached back to the switch panel (housing 90 switches in all) on the after-wheelhouse face and calmly, without apparently looking, selected the correct switch at the first attempt and doused the lights. The look on Duncan Forester's face was a picture and his exclamation of "How the hell did you know that Pilot?" was understandable.

"You don't remember me, do you Captain Forester?" I replied, and he had to say that he didn't. I quickly put him out of his misery and we started to reminisce and bemoan the obvious sad decline of such a wonderful company as Blue Funnel. Of course, the company was still in existence at that time but I could tell, sadly, that things were not all 'rosy in the garden'. We chatted for a few more minutes and then the Chief Officer appeared from his standby station at the bows of the ship (known as the the foc's'le), where he had been controlling the unmooring of the ship and attending to the tugs' wires for the departure manoeuvre. It was his vital job throughout the operation to safely control the mooring lines and keep the deck crew that were with him, safe. He was discussing things with his Captain and I was completely pre-occupied with doing my job of safely guiding the ship down the river by issuing courses to steer to the man on the wheel and adjusting the ship's speed, keeping her well within the channels that are notoriously fickle on the River Humber.

While I was carrying out this 'conning' as it is known, I was aware that the Chief Officer was looking at me in a sideways sort of fashion and I returned his embarrassed glance just as shamefacedly, as it had become obvious that we knew each other but couldn't remember each other's names.

Finally, he broke the ice and said, "Excuse me Pilot, I can't help feeling I know you from somewhere." I replied that I was feeling exactly the same and, lo and behold, it was Peter Finch – we had signed indentures and started in the company as apprenticed Midshipmen on the same day, 9th October 1961, and here we were, some 20 years later, on the same ship for the first time since we started in the company. Of course, our roles had altered somewhat – him still the company employee, and me, well that's another story. We reminisced for some time and swapped stories of the good old days and chatted at length about colleagues that we had both known and who had also departed the fold of the mighty Ocean Fleets as the company had become known, to prosper or otherwise, elsewhere.

I really enjoyed that trip down the river. Sadly, it was the one and only time that I piloted a true 'Blue Flue' vessel. I had seen them while training on the river and then again whilst completing my four years as an 'under draft' man in the capacity of Third- and then Second-Class Humber Pilot, where the ships of the size of the *Patroclus* were too deep for me to be let loose on, and I hadn't gained sufficient experience to pilot them. Apart from once taking an Elder Dempster Line ship (part of the Ocean Fleets Group) into Immingham, that was the only occasion that I felt 'back home' as it were.

The one thing that sticks in my mind about the whole episode is that when Duncan Forester realised that I had only been Second Officer on that class of ship, his ship that I was now piloting, and on further probing discovered that I have never actually handled a Glenalmond-class ship before, that's when it came out: "Bloody hell Pilot, you might've told me!"

Patroclus – 12,082 gross tons – 14,182 dead-weight tons.
One of the eight Priam- and Glenalmond-class ships.

Lern Yerself Scouse
(With apologies to Fritz Spiegl)

When, in October 1961, I joined Alfred Holt and Company's Blue Funnel and Glen Lines as an indentured apprenticed Midshipman, I have to admit that I was very naïve. Until I went to Aberdovey to attend an Outward Bound Sea School training course in August of the same year, I had never heard an accent other than that of my native Yorkshire, and it was at Aberdovey that I came into contact with many differing accents and brogues, 'Geordie' being the strangest of the ones that I encountered on that 26-day course in 1961 that we had to undertake and successfully complete before being offered an apprenticeship with, and accepted into, the Blue Funnel Line.

But probably the biggest shock of my life was to come when I joined my first deep sea ship, the *Aeneas*, and I came closely into contact with 'Scousers'. Alfred Holt and Company had a strong tradition of training not only their young Midshipmen and Officers, but they also had their own pool of dedicated seafarers who manned the ships of the company and were treated as 'family', much as we aspiring young men were as well. The reputation of the owners was such that they engendered loyalty and devotion and paid above the odds to the normal seamen of the day. Thus, where many of the ships of the Merchant Navy of the day were manned by a 'hotch potch' of men 'from the pool' (the pet name for the Shipping Federation) Blue Funnel ships were manned by company men who were loyal to their employers and mainly from Liverpool itself, or from Wales. 'Blueys' or 'The China Boats', as they were known, were considered the unofficial Welsh

Navy as a large contingent of men came from that lovely land over the border who brought with them their own traditions and ways of doing things.

Anchises, sister ship to the *Aeneas* – Standard 'A'-class Blue Funnel ship that were the backbone of the fleet built after the heavy losses during World War 2.

However, the main bulk of seamen came from Liverpool itself and brought to the sea their own inimitable accent and wonderful sense of humour. Many years later, when a Humber Pilot, I was invited to a Liverpool Pilot's Retirement Hot Pot evening by some colleagues, and as there were quite a few retirements to be observed during that particular evening, one of my hosts apologised for there not being the usual comedian to entertain during the course of the proceedings. Once the retirement speeches got going, it was absolutely apparent that they didn't need the services of a comedian at all – the Liverpool Pilots themselves have an inborn sense of humour and required no assistance at all!

But the Petty Officers, Able Seamen and all the lower ranks of the crews on the ships I served on brought such fun to the job of being at sea that the long time spent away from home was lightened by their 'devil may care' attitude and their sheer determination not to let anything get them down. Liverpool-based jokes abounded and were always good-natured punts at their style of communicating and prods at their way of life. Like the one about the two Liverpool seamen sitting in their smoke room on the ship far from home, one reading a copy of *Playboy* (the seamen's Bible) and the other writing a letter home to his mum. The letter writer turned to his mate and asked, "Hey der La', how do you spell 'Darrel'?" The *Playboy* reader, mystified, turned and asked back, "Whaddya mean 'Darrel'?" The letter writer replied, "You know, I'm writing home to me mam and I want 'er to knit me a pair of socks Darrel fit me!" "Oh you daft bugger," replied the other, "it's not 'Darrel', its Worral!"

There were many instances of this self-effacing humour where these fine men were absolutely honest about their roots and they had no 'airs and graces' at all. But woe betide anyone who tried to be 'a bit clever' with them. A fair proportion of the ships in the company were manned by Chinese ratings, mainly in the engineering and catering departments. As Deck Officers we had no real contact with the engine room ratings, but we came into close contact with the Chinese stewards who were employed to clean our cabins and serve us our meals. A Chinese steward, when taking your order for a complete meal, would hover while we selected our repast from the menu cards that were in the dining saloon, and then bring us our next selection once we had finished our previous course. However, if you had a Liverpool steward, he would take the order for one course at a time and ask you in between each course for your next selection.

On one occasion we had a rather 'clever' young junior engineer who joined the ship, full of the virtue of the Chinese stewards he had previously sailed with on another of the company's ships, and seemed determined to have a go at the much slower British steward serving at the engineers' table. When he was presented with the menu for the meal, he ordered all four courses at the same time, grinning to the other engineers sitting at the table with him and pronouncing that he would see if this Scouser could cope. When his soup course, fish course, main course and pudding, complete with a scoop of ice cream atop the latter, arrived all on the same soup plate, I have to admit that he took it in his stride. The engineer simply removed the ice cream from the tip of the enormous pile of food, placed it on his side plate, and consumed the meal amid smiles from his colleagues at the table. He didn't try that again!

The brushes with this keen sense of humour continued throughout my career, and many years later when I was Master of the *Hullgate* (the tanker I commanded for a while before being accepted into the Humber Pilot Service) I encountered another Liverpool lad with that wonderful sense of the ridiculous. Life on the *Hullgate* was a totally different world to that which I had been used to, and one of my duties was to calculate and pay the wages of the crew in cash every week. There were many little rules that applied to bonuses and extras that the crew could be entitled to, one of which was compensation for disturbed sleep should any crew member have to be called out during the night before he had taken a minimum of four hours sleep. As one can imagine on a coastal tanker shuttling between ports in the

UK, this happened quite often, and when sifting through the overtime and extra payment claims that the individual seamen had to submit each week before I could calculate how much they were owed, I came across this magic request for 'L.O.D.' Never to be outdone, this great lad from Bootle (on Merseyside), when quizzed, simply replied, "Crikey Skipper, don't you know – that's for 'Loss of Doss'!"

My first ship to sea, the *Aeneas*, was crewed by Liverpool sailors and Petty Officers, but the catering department was manned by Chinese staff recruited via the company's manning agency in Hong Kong, again 'company men' who were as loyal to the owners as were their English and Welsh counterparts. I had to quickly learn a manner of speaking to these stewards in 'Pidgin English', aided by the Senior Midshipmen on the ship, and I quickly learned to speak in this slightly bizarre fashion to the lads in the galley and the saloon. On completing my first deep sea voyage of some five and a half months duration from the UK to Indonesia and back, I was then appointed to a coasting trip on a more modern ship, the *Antenor*, sailing from Liverpool after discharging her cargo there, and proceeding to Glasgow, Hamburg and Rotterdam, discharging and loading before returning to Birkenhead to complete her loading for departure for the Far East once more. The *Antenor* was manned by a Liverpool crew on deck and in the catering department, but these lads had been sent home for their leave and the galley staff were replaced by Chinese staff for the duration of the coastal trip.

A part of the Junior Midshipman's work was keeping the halfdeck (the Midshipmen's accommodation) clean and also stocked with tea, coffee, milk and sugar for brewing at 'smoko time', the breaks in the daily routine of running the ship. The supplies for these duties had to be obtained from the mess boy in the galley, and before sailing from Liverpool I went to the galley to find a very Chinese looking young lad hovering about. So, putting on my best Pidgin Chinese accent, I launched into my request for tea, coffee, milk etc. saying, "Excuse me, can do tea, coffee, sugar, milk for Midshipmen for makey smoko and cloth, brush, soap for cleany halfdeck, OK?"

This outburst was met with a rather stunned reply, "Are yews OK der La'?"

Mystified, I obtained the stores and on returning to the halfdeck with my spoils, enquired of the others what was going on.

"Oh they'll all be from the Liverpool Chinese community of catering staff that live here in Liverpool to relieve the lads when the ship docks!"

Over the years Chinese crew had jumped ship in Liverpool and mingled with and married into the local community, and there was, and still is, a huge Chinese population contributing to the verve of life within Merseyside. Much egg on my face that day!

But probably one of the funniest tales that circulated in the company was the story of the sailor on one of the passenger carrying ships that ran to Australia from Liverpool. These four Blue Funnel 'H'-class ships, the *Helenus, Hector, Ixion* and *Jason* carried 36 passengers in luxury between the UK and the Antipodes, and appointment to these ships was considered to be a bonus within the company – something I personally never aspired to! The *Ixion* was affectionately known among the Liverpool crews as the '9-to-1 on' – a play on words relating to betting odds and yet another example of the intelligent humour of the fine crews employed within the company. However, the joke relates to the evening when one of the sailors was on his way up to the bridge to collect the Third Officer's teapot from the wheelhouse to take down to the mess to make him his 10 o'clock tea. On his way up to the bridge of the ship this sailor had to pass the promenade deck where the passengers' cabins were situated. It was a strict rule within the company that junior officers and sailors were not allowed to converse or mix with passengers, but if approached and asked a question, they should politely attempt to answer. On this particular occasion an elderly lady passenger was leaning on the ship's rail gazing up at the stars. As the sailor passed her, she accosted him and asked, "Excuse me, can you tell me what that group of stars is up there and in particular that very bright star associated with it?" The sailor replied that he didn't know but would ask the officer of the watch and tell her when he came back down again.

Jason, One of the four 'H'-class ships that ran to Australia from Liverpool.

On arriving at the bridge, the sailor dutifully asked the Third Officer the question, and the officer explained that the stars were the constellation of Orion, and the bright star was Sirius. Making sure the sailor had the information correctly ingrained into his head, he repeated, "Now have you got that? Explain the rough trapezium shape of the constellation and that if you follow the line of Orion's 'belt' out of the constellation you come to that very bright star, which is the brightest star in the sky, and its name is Sirius – OK?" Nodding, the sailor collected the teapot and made his way down to the promenade deck with this information stored in his head. But sadly, the information came out somewhat haphazardly, and when the passenger asked again, he simply replied, "Oh yeah, I asked the Third Officer and he said that 'erm, oh yeah, that's the constipation of O'Brien, and that's Seeerious."

Constellation of Orion and Sirius.

The 'Duck'

The transition from operating conventional ships over water at sedate speeds and the ways of travelling across the sea at high speed was a difficulty that had to be overcome when entering the brave new world of the hovercraft industry. In the heady, early days of the development of that wonderful way of travel, there was a belief that this was the new 'coming' world of high-speed travel, and the introduction to it was a challenge. We 'new' Commanders had to 'cut our teeth' in this new world, and we did so on the Hovermarine HM2 'sidewall' hovercraft.

The early hovercraft were complicated beasts with sophisticated airframe construction methods and gas turbine engines which were light and powerful, but expensive to build and operate. Why not build a simpler vehicle using conventional marine methods that could travel across the water? So, the idea of the Hovermarine 'HM2' series was born. What was planned was a simple flat-bottomed boat, 52-feet long and 19-feet wide, that you stuck an upside down 'biscuit tin' on the bottom of. You then knocked out the two shorter ends around bow and stern, substituted flexible rubber skirts to contain an air cushion, and bunged some diesel engines in it. Simple and cheap to manufacture; you were on to a winner.

So, the Hovermarine HM2 was born. Great idea for a craft that could carry 65 passengers across sheltered water crossings at speeds between 35 and 40 knots, operating from conventional berths that were already there at Portsmouth Harbour Station and Ryde Pier. SeaSpeed (British Rail Hovercraft Ltd.) chartered and operated HM2 *001* for a season in 1968, and after several teething problems they ordered two more for themselves – *004* and *007*. SeaSpeed was initially set up to operate new designs of hovercraft for manufacturers, and to trial them in real passenger-carrying roles. The idea was brilliant, a lot cheaper to operate than the sophisticated amphibious craft that were being produced by the British Hovercraft Corporation in Cowes on the Isle of Wight, which SeaSpeed operated on their Cowes to Southampton route. But like any brilliant idea, the transition of brainwave to end product via drawing board and manufacture was fraught with obstacles, and the beloved plastic 'Duck' as it was affectionally nicknamed suffered more than most!

Bare HM2 fibreglass shell ready for fitting out.

The early models suffered from all sorts of problems and, although mostly solved over a period of time, I saw the Mark 1 craft with all their shortcomings and the ingenious ways the Commanders of those days overcame them. In 1970, the manufacturers, Hovermarine, took on board all the criticisms made by the Commanders and crews, and set about solving most of them. Some were technical shortcomings which they solved very simply, but the main complaints were the amount of noise in the passenger compartment due to oversimplified drive trains between engines, gearboxes and propellors, making it very noisy and uncomfortable within the passenger cabin. Thus, was born the Mark 3 in the guise of the first production SeaSpeed craft – *001* – being taken back and heavily modified into the Mark 3 – renumbered HM2 *301*. Gear boxes and transfer drives were changed for more highly engineered 'off the shelf' Italian 'V'-drive derivatives which were quieter and much sweeter running, almost eliminating the vibrations that reverberated through the craft which caused discomfort for the passengers. The *301* was a truly different machine to the Mark 1!

One of the worst features of the craft was the tendency for it to 'plough in' – a nasty habit where, when the very simple bow skirt hit a large wave or a ship's wash, it would flick back and cause the craft to nose dive, hitting the water and stopping rather quickly. A bit disconcerting for passengers and crew alike! The solution was a much modified and fuller bow skirt, which billowed out in front of the craft giving much more support and a much more comfortable ride. So SeaSpeed decided to have their two craft – *004* and *007* – fitted with the new skirt to improve the ride. Sadly, being British Rail, they decided against the new gearboxes and transfer drives to the propellors because of the cost, so the noise problem continued, pushed on to the back burner by British Rail, as they considered the journey time between Portsmouth and Ryde being only 10 minutes was too short for it to be worried about.

Rather short sighted, but there we were, and I started my official training in March 1971 and commenced as a

'Temporary' Hovercraft Commander for the summer season shortly afterwards.

The craft soldiered on and established a route that today is served by fast catamarans, not as speedy as the original hovercraft, but faster than the original sedate passenger ferries which took 45 to 50 minutes to do the crossing.

HM2 *004* 'on cushion' and being manoeuvred off the berth at Portsmouth. The water line 'off cushion' is where the white line below the Seaspeed logo is placed, and the craft simply rises onto its cushion clear of the water when the lift engine is throttled up.

The craft were similar to a hydrofoil in many ways; the big difference being that the hydrofoil needed a fair amount of forward speed to 'lift itself' onto its skis or foils to ride above the waves, whereas, as can be seen from the photo above, the HM2 lifted herself up when air was pushed into the air cushion.

I had been associated with the set up in SeaSpeed for quite a time as my long-standing and very good friend, with whom I had been at sea with in Blue Funnel, was already a Commander with the outfit. In my limited time off between voyages away from home at sea while I completed the required qualifying time before sitting for my Masters exams, I had spent many happy hours travelling back and forth between Portsmouth and Ryde on the Hovermarine HM2s operated by SeaSpeed. I had been 'unofficially' taught all there was to know about the machines, so after passing my Masters Foreign Going Certificate after an intense period of study in early 1971, encouraged by my friend, I applied to SeaSpeed in the spring of 1971 and started my official training. Thanks to my new friends I was well prepared to take on the role.

Thus, I commenced four of the happiest years of my working life 'charging around on the big puff of wind!'

Most of the ancillary problems with the HM2 still existed, and now it was my turn to deal with them. Fortunately, we had with us on the flight deck a Coxswain whose duties included actually steering the craft in foggy conditions while the Commander had his eyes and head in the radar, conning the craft. These fine chaps had worked on the craft for three years before I started with the company, and thankfully were there to give advice when things went a bit wrong! Windscreen wipers and washers were always packing up – rather essential when travelling at speed and the windows became spattered with the inevitable spray that occurred when we lifted the craft up on to its cushion of air. Solution – for the former problem of the wiper motor or gearbox giving up the ghost – two pieces of 'technical' string attached to the wiper arms, one bit of string out of each of the side windows of the flight deck pulled alternately to provide the wiping action! Very sophisticated, but it worked until the engineers, who were constantly being called out, appeared to fix the problem! The window washer problem was solved with equal sophistication and washing-up liquid bottles filled with water were brandished out through the sliding side windows of the cockpit and the contents squirted at the windows to remove any salt stains that were inevitably and frequently obscuring the view out of the front windows of the craft. The latter solution was OK in the summer months but having to do this in the winter months was no joke!

We sometimes wondered what the passengers would have thought if they knew just what was being done to keep the craft running in all weathers and also to keep them safe. But they kept coming and I spent two very happy years flashing back and forth between Portsmouth Harbour Station Pier and Ryde Pier, nursing the 'Duck' until SeaSpeed decided enough was enough, and the service was terminated at the end of 1972. At the culmination of the first season in 1971 on the HM2, myself and two of my other colleagues, John Summers and Ken Blackwood, were interviewed for permanent positions within the company, and we commenced our training on the much more sophisticated SRN6 amphibious machines – a whole new ball game!

HM2 *301* at speed during Department of Trade trials.

The Price of a Box of Cauliflowers

In the early days of my career as a Pilot on the Humber, the whole of the estuary (for the Humber is an estuary – not a river in the true sense of the word) was split into three separate Pilotage districts. These were the Lower Station Humber men of whom I was one, the Goole Pilotage area which comprised inward and outward Pilots, and the River Trent Pilots. There was no real rivalry between the different districts as the style of piloting and ship handling were, of necessity, totally at odds with the other districts in the overall area. The 'up river' men bounced their way over the river bed to Goole and the berths on the River Trent, whereas the Lower Station men handled much larger ships and were respectful of the fact that you just didn't touch the bottom with a large ship as the consequences could be dire.

Later on, of course as a supposed money-saving exercise we did, at the behest of the port authority, combine or amalgamate the three services together to get rid of the launch that was used to change Pilots over in Hull Roads, the channel immediately adjacent to the port of Hull. Prior to that we in the Lower Station would fetch the inward-bound ships as far as Hull Roads, and there await the pleasure of the Goole or Trent men who would come off from the pier at Hull on the launch, and relieve us, taking their charges onwards to their berths in the upper reaches.

On the Lower Station boarding position at sea, there was some semblance of order as to which Pilot would be allocated to each ship that was coming inward, although this could be fraught with so many rules that it was understandable that we often were confused and would end up on the 'wrong ship', bound for somewhere we weren't expecting to go, but restrictions allowing, we did usually end up with the right ship and all was calm, cool and collected; well as much as could be expected!

However, the up-river men – particularly the Goole men – would leave the allocation of the ships until they actually joined the launch at Hull to go off to board the ships as they arrived. The Trent men usually had things sorted before they joined the launch, and what would ensue was sometimes amusing, but often a bit annoying for us Lower Station men, who would be trying to avoid running into the ship ahead of us in the queue, with a strong current behind us whooshing us up the river and making the ship somewhat uncontrollable. We would also be repeatedly asking whether the Goole man wanted the ship turned around to 'stem the inrushing tide' to await more depth of water before he could proceed on his way to the upper reaches. Often, no reply would be forthcoming and confusion could, and did, sometimes reign!

It all added to the fun of the job, but I digress. When I first started life on the river, the outside influences on the fees that we earned for each act of pilotage we carried out had a nasty habit of fluctuating incredibly wildly; often our money received at the end of the month would vary by huge sums, depending on how many ships we, as a group, had handled during that month. The salary construction was actually non-existent in normal terms. All the monies earned by the Pilots during the month were collected into one large pot and divided up. A First-Class Pilot would receive a full share, a Second-Class Pilot four-fifths of a share, and a Third-Class Pilot three-fifths of a share. However, the overall earning capacity of the pot would depend on how many ships we'd handled during that particular month, and things could vary enormously. And here comes the 'rub' – there were the other factors as well over which we had absolutely no control. The steel workers' dispute of the '70s, the lorry drivers' and dockers' disputes of the '70s and '80s plus the huge coal miners' dispute of the '80s and numerous other factors would, could, and did affect the income for not just the Lower Station, but the Upper Stations as well.

In order to survive, many Pilots took on other jobs or businesses. The Lower Station Pilots were somewhat restricted in that they could not devote their time to other methods of earning as easily as others on the river, as they worked the river and the ports 'round the clock' and, more importantly, at most states of the tide, whereas the upper reaches were very tidal and could not be worked at low water. However, we all did manage to survive.

Myself, I ran a small tree-felling business for some years in my days off, to feed the fires in my own house and to supplement my income. Another colleague used to do painting and decorating, but the main protagonists of the extracurricular activities were the upriver men who turned their hands to all sorts. One ran a thriving curtain shop and fitting business along with his wife, and another a small fishing tackle shop in Goole. Another had a small former fishing boat that he used to take fishing parties out on to the river, and which also appeared in the famous *Only Fools and Horses* episode, *To Hull and Back*. However, probably one of the more successful and prosperous Goole Pilots ran initially one greengrocer's shop, and later he expanded to two shops. This snowballed somewhat and gave him and his wife a very comfortable life, even though he had to work long hours and 'fit in' his work on the river. He would be in the Hull fruit and vegetable market in the early hours, buying stock and negotiating with the fruit merchants who got to know and respect him for a very keen businessman who didn't allow them to pull the wool over his eyes. Although the fruit market in Hull was almost adjacent to the Hull Pilot Office where Pilots would gather before going off to their ships, it still entailed this budding entrepreneurial greengrocer with some worries and long hours.

This all came to fruition (if you'll pardon the pun) one morning on the launch in Hull Roads. At the time, the normal channel immediately adjacent to Hull had silted up at its upper end and had closed. This entailed ALL the upriver Pilots having to join the launch and proceed across the shallow part of the river off Hull to the 'South Channel' near the opposite side of the river off New Holland in Lincolnshire. One of my more senior colleagues had brought a ship up to Hull Roads for an early boarding for Gainsborough, some 40 miles further up the river and as far as any seagoing ship could possibly proceed. He had handed over his charge to the Trent Pilot who had already proceeded on his way and was sitting on the launch while the other ships arrived to be boarded. The Goole Pilots were in their usual state of confusion, and were discussing the pros and cons of each ship, which berth it was going to in Goole, and what draft the ship was – none of this being carried out in any apparent orderly manner and being a total mystery to my senior colleague, who incidentally was in for a bit of a wait before being taken back to the pier at Hull and being able to proceed home!

All the more senior Goole men were seemingly bandying ships backwards and forwards between themselves and arguing which would be best for themselves, except for this one Goole Pilot who sat impassively on the seats in the launch, taking absolutely no part at all in these discussions. Slightly baffled, my senior colleague leant across to this Pilot and asked him, "Dennis, don't you take any part in this vital meeting about which ship you should take?"

The greengrocer, for that was who this Pilot was, merely looked my colleague straight in the eye and replied, "To be quite honest Ken, just point me at a ship and put me on it and I'll do it, I'll take it anywhere, I don't really care. To be absolutely frank, all I'm worried about this morning is the price of a box of cauliflowers!"

40-foot Halmatic Pilot launch – *Fox* – The type commonly used in Hull Roads for the transfer of Lower and Upper Station Pilots.

Around the World in 114 Days

Sea time was at a premium for all Merchant Navy officers and Midshipmen, and in order to be eligible to sit for professional examinations to advance your career, you had to complete so much 'time at sea'. The three-and-a-half-year indentured apprenticeship that I signed with Alfred Holt and Company required me to complete 36 months at sea before being eligible to sit for my Second Mates Certificate of Competency, and thus progress to the dizzy height of Extra Third Officer within the company. So, to achieve this rather long period at sea actually signed on to the articles of ships, the Midshipmen's Department in Blue Funnel used to allocate us to what was commonly termed as a 'Long Jag' – an extended voyage 'around the world' on one of the ships that never came 'home'.

We had several ships within the fleet attached to the Barber Blue Sea Line, a conglomerate of different companies' ships that traded between the Far East and the mighty United States of America. Masters, Chief Engineers, Chief Officers and Second Engineers would fly to the States to join the ships in New York, and the more junior ship's officers would travel in style on Cunard Line passenger ships across the Atlantic. However, we lowly Midshipmen would 'work' our passage to the Far East on a main line ship of the company, and transfer to these 'Round the World' ships that never came 'home' to the UK, relieving our counterparts in Hong Kong who would then travel home again, working their passage back to the UK on the main line ship.

So, it came about that in 1963 I was allocated to the *Telamon* for an extended period of service to boost my sea time towards completing my apprenticeship. The *Telamon* was one of three ships that were not initially built for the Blue Funnel Line, rather they were 'bought on the stocks' as a 'cancelled' order from another British shipping company, Silver Line, and were not typical of the robust construction or standard of the regular 'Blueys'. I sailed from London on the *Glenearn* with Captain Millbank in command and my three other Midshipmen colleagues to travel to the Far East to join the *Telamon* in Hong Kong, and relieve the other Middies on *Telamon* who had completed their extended trip abroad. One of the early memories of that trip out to the Far East that sticks in my mind was that while on bridge standby as we were leaving London, the Captain asked me where I was from. When I told him, it turned out that he also was from Kingston upon Hull, and on further chatting discovered that he knew and had been a boyfriend of my own mother back in the distant past before her marriage to my father! Slightly embarrassing but liveable with.

TSMV *Glenearn*, our transport to the Far East.
Photo courtesy of the late Ted Aughey.

The Chief Officer of the *Glenearn* was a rather infamous character known as 'Alehouse Evans', an officer who had come up 'through the hawsepipe' as it was known then. This was a very difficult route for any member of the deck crew and was regarded as a great achievement. Unlike the slightly more cosseted Midshipmen of the day, these lads from the deck crew had to strive and struggle to gain the high ranks, and 'Alehouse' had succeeded with grit and determination. The term 'coming up through the hawsepipe' refers to the practice many moons ago when pirates and other ne'er do wells would scale the anchor chain from the waterline when a ship was anchored, pass through the hawsepipe – a pipe from deck of a ship to the water through which the anchor chain passed, and thus gain access for naughty deeds via the most difficult and dangerous method imaginable.

He had started his career as a Deck Boy with Blue Funnel and had immediately aspired to becoming an officer. The company encouraged that track for any of its deck crew who so wished and had set up a fund – the 'Calchas Fund' – to encourage and financially support these aspirations. 'Alehouse', as he was affectionately known, had a reputation as a somewhat heavy drinker, and had apparently on one occasion when on leave returned home from the pub to be asked by his wife where the baby was? He had taken the baby for a walk in her pram and left her parked outside an inn while he went in for a 'quickie'. With him living in rural Wales there was no problem – the baby was returned home a very short while afterwards after being discovered by another regular at the pub, none the worse for her ordeal! He was nevertheless highly respected as a good Chief Officer who knew his job inside out and was very diligent and conscientious.

We had a very heavy lift to discharge from *Glenearn* in Singapore outward bound, and on inspection it was found that the foot brake on one of the winches for the heavy lift derrick was somewhat seized up with many layers of paint on it. Undeterred, Alehouse set about rectifying the problem, and as I was working alongside him at the time, he asked me to go to his office and retrieve a sample bottle of a cargo we were carrying at the time. This cargo was a liquid chemical that had been loaded in Middlesbrough for shipping to Japan, with a trade name of 'Dobane'. He had discovered quite by accident during a previous voyage that this substance was a marvellous 'freeing agent' which could work miracles on seized and rusted nuts and bolts and anything else that had succumbed to the salt water environment that was life on a ship. Returning with this glass bottle of strange-looking clear liquid chemical, we drizzled a few drops onto the seized mechanism of the foot brake, and moments later the paint started to sizzle and drop off in lumps. It certainly worked as the brake became totally operational again and the lift was discharged without any mishaps. On doing some research we discovered that this chemical was in fact an additive to soap powder manufactured in Japan, and the thought immediately crossed everyone's minds: if it did that to rust and paint, what would it do to your underpants!

We arrived in Hong Kong and left the *Glenearn*, transferring to the *Telamon* in Taikoo Dry Dock where she was having a 'spruce up' and relieved our counterparts to travel onward and then homeward on the *Glenearn*.

Telamon's schedule commenced 'empty' in Hong Kong in dry dock, then down to the Philippines to load 5,000 tons of sugar in bulk for one of the many sugar wharves in the States, returning to Hong Kong to continue loading manufactured goods, then up to Japan to complete loading before crossing the Pacific. The *Telamon* and her two sisters *Teucer* and *Telemachus* were steam turbine ships that consumed about

90 tons of fuel per day in their thirsty boilers, and she could just make it to San Pedro, Los Angeles, to replenish her oil tanks after the 14-day passage across the Pacific Ocean. Refuelled, she would then transit the Panama Canal into the Caribbean, calling at Kingston, Jamaica before proceeding to her 'home port' of New York. Discharging and loading then took place down the eastern seaboard of America and into the Gulf of Mexico, visiting places such as Boston, Philadelphia, Charleston, Houston, Galveston, New Orleans and on that trip, Baton Rouge, after a tortuous passage up the mighty Mississippi River.

We mingled with the locals and tried to soak up the American way of life, but being Middies on a minute salary, our pleasures had to be of the more frugal type. Whilst discharging the sugar in Philadelphia, I proceeded ashore one night in the baking heat to take in a movie at the local air-conditioned cinema, as the ship did not have the luxury of air conditioning, and it was very hot at the time in Pennsylvania. Bearing in mind that as Middies we were not allowed to drink alcohol as we would break the archaic terms of our indentures, I stopped off at a very small dockland bar on the way back to the ship. When I entered, I didn't actually notice, but on approaching the bar to buy a beer, the bartender came and stood right in front of me with his arms outspread on the bar counter and simply fixed me with a rather menacing stare. With the hairs on the back of my neck starting to bristle uncomfortably, the penny dropped that he and all the occupants of the bar were African Americans. Being slightly concerned for my safety, I merely apologised and started to retreat towards the door. However, on speaking in my English accent, the look on the bartender's face changed and he simply asked, "You a Limey?" to which I simply answered, "Yes."

"Siddown" was the retort and I eventually left that bar somewhat worse for wear at about 3 o'clock the following morning after being quizzed in detail about the progressive English attitude towards the black community in our country, and I never bought a beer all that night! I learnt a lot about the so-called relaxing of the rules regarding the colour bar that operated in those days of 1960's America and it was something of an eye opener.

While in Philadelphia there was an incident that had started back in Kingston, Jamaica, when we had called there to discharge part of our cargo. Arriving there we noticed a Canadian warship alongside at a berth near to us, and that same evening, three of her crew came to visit. They had heard of the legendary service that Blue Funnel Line ships had given during the 2nd World War and wanted to have a look round to see for themselves. Even though *Telamon* was not a typical Blue Funnel design, they nonetheless were impressed when I showed them the bridge and around the decks after I was delegated to be their guide. During conversation with them, they discovered that it was my 18th birthday the following day, and I was formally invited to join them at lunchtime for 'sippers' – the Royal Naval tradition of everyone sharing their tot of rum from their daily issue with any guests that were attending. Not being allowed to drink on board any of the company's ships, I eagerly accepted their invitation, and with permission from the Chief Officer to 'go ashore' I went aboard the Canadian warship to sample their hospitality. Returning to the ship at about 1500 after imbibing what was to me an overdose of strong Navy rum, I was immediately required to join in a stowaway search on the *Telamon* before we sailed that evening. This was necessary as the lure of stowing away and then jumping ship in New York was too much for the local Jamaicans to resist.

Joining the search, I was asked to climb up onto one of the two yachts destined for owners in America that we had carried on deck from Hong Kong where they had been built. One was a copy of a traditional Chinese junk, carefully and lovingly built of the finest wood available – cost being no object – and I shinned up the outside of the crate that this beautiful replica was encased in. After searching, I then proceeded to climb down again, but lost my footing and fell about ten feet to the deck of the ship, but avoided any injury as I was probably somewhat worse for wear and just went totally limp. Unfortunately, when we arrived in New York, the immigration guard stationed at the top of our ship's gangway discovered a stowaway trying to sneak ashore, and all hell was let loose. We never found out where he had secreted himself on the ship in Jamaica, but there had always been that nagging doubt in my own mind that I had missed him when I searched.

The authorities insisted that we lock this stowaway up in the brig (the prison or secure cell on a ship) that they fancifully expected us to have on board, which of course we didn't have, so the only alternative was to keep him corralled in the Tally Clerk's office on deck, situated in the mast house between two of the hatches. These mast houses were strongly built steel structures that were between each of the hatches to provide a strong seating and base for the masts that carried the ship's derricks (cranes) and were used for store rooms and cargo offices. They all had secure doors which could be locked, but were very basic and uncomfortable, not being designed to be lived in. Immigration guards were enforced and a second separate guard was positioned outside the locked steel door of this office to ensure he didn't escape ashore. This worked OK in

New York, but on arrival in Philadelphia there was a great amount of unease amongst the predominantly coloured stevedores, and they actually went on strike, refusing to work the ship unless this poor unfortunate chap was released from the 'cell' that he was being kept in. A period of impasse followed, but then the situation was mysteriously resolved on the second evening of our stay there, as this chap managed to escape from his incarceration, probably with help from some of his sympathisers among the stevedoring community. The ship, however, was still fined heavily under American immigration violation laws, and the incident came to an end.

Later in that trip around the coast of America, the beautiful Hong Kong built junk had to be discharged in Charleston, South Carolina. We were due to unload it to a low loader on the quay and with it weighing in at some 14 tons, it required not only the use of our 25-ton heavy lift derrick at No 4 hatch, but also the special wire slings that were to be attached to the reinforced crate that the junk was stowed in. These slings had been provided in Hong Kong from Blue Funnel's own rigging works that were a part of the service we provided in the Far East. American stevedores have their own incredibly powerful Teamster unions, and their representative on board refused to allow us to discharge this heavy lift unless we used their own rather tatty looking slings that they had brought on board. Our Chief Officer refused point blank, which brought about another stand-off, which was only resolved after much negotiation between our agent and the boss of the Teamsters. Eventually it was agreed that they could use their own slings providing that they signed a letter stating that any damage caused would be their responsibility and that no blame could be apportioned to the ship. The owner of the new junk who had attended on board the ship to see his pride and joy was unhappy with this arrangement, but if we were to ever sail, this compromise had to be agreed. Indeed, he was reluctant to let the stevedores use their own slings but had to agree under pressure from his countrymen.

On lifting the junk from the deck it was obvious to all that these dodgy slings weren't up to the job as they started to make some alarming noises, but the stevedores insisted we carry on with the lift, and on swinging the yacht over the quay, fortunately before the low loader positioned itself under the suspended yacht, one of the slings started to 'strand off' and then the inevitable sadly happened. ('Stranding off' occurs when one of the multiple strands that make up a large heavy wire rope sling fails, and the weight is transferred to the remaining strands. When they can't support the strain after the first strand has broken, they all break in turn, giving some audible warning of the impending failure of the rope sling. If caught early enough in the lifting process of a heavy lift, the lift can be lowered quickly back onto the deck of the ship without causing any catastrophe, but sadly in this case it didn't happen.)

The other slings couldn't take the extra strain and, crashing down on to the quay, the yacht didn't stand a chance – the beautiful yacht we had so lovingly cared for on its journey from the other side of the world ended up as so much matchwood.

Three representatives of the stevedore's union tried to divert blame away from themselves, but the agent had thoughtfully filmed the whole operation from the upper deck of the ship on a cine camera, something we had never seen before, and when showed the evidence, they had to back off and accept full responsibility for the 'accident'. It took a while for the clear up on the jetty, but they did clear it up and it was sad to see the remains of that beautiful junk replica yacht being carted away in several dumpsters, as the Americans call skips.

When we finally left the American coast after our discharge and reload, we proceeded across the Atlantic towards the Mediterranean and Alexandria – our first discharge port on our continuing trip around the world. During our final stay in New York to complete loading before continuing eastwards on our voyage, the weather was still very humid and incredibly hot, and for entertainment we would go ashore to the centre of the city to view the sights. With it being so hot, I put on some cooler gear comprising some shorts and a short-sleeved shirt to go ashore, and on boarding the 'underground' (which in New York runs above the streets on raised tracks on stilts), I didn't detect any problem, although I sensed that I was being looked at rather strangely. On arriving in Times Square and taking in the hustle and bustle of the rat race that was New York, a police car drew up alongside me, the rear door was opened remotely from inside the cabin, and I was 'requested' to, "Get in Bud!"

The two New York policemen stared at me in the caged rear section of the car from their places in the front seats of the vehicle, and asked what I thought I was doing? Mystified I had no answer at first, but on enquiring in my normal British accent, they exclaimed, "Oh Gawd, a Limey!" They then educated me that it was, at that time, illegal to wear shorts on the streets of downtown New York City. I professed my absolute ignorance of this rule, and they looked at each other rather exasperatedly, asked where I was staying and when I explained that I was from a ship in the docks and had travelled in on the subway, they took pity on me and I have to say were very generous. They took me all the way back to Manhattan in their police car to where the ship was berthed, waited while I went aboard and changed into more appropriate gear, and then ran me all the way back to Times Square, dropping me off where they had arrested me in the first place! New York's finest as they say.

During the long night security watches that we, as Midshipmen were expected to carry out while the ship was in New York, we used to listen to the radio a lot. We had a particularly good radio in our accommodation on that ship, left over by some previous Middies who had served there before us. It was a famous radio of the day – a Pye Cambridge – not particularly expensive but of very good British quality and soundly made. One of my cohorts on that extended trip, Don McReary, had in fact done a school exchange between his school in England and a school in New York. He was therefore conversant with the radio stations in the city, and he tuned in the radio to WINS, a station that belted out pop music around the clock, playing all the hits of the day and taking requests from all and sundry. Sitting there one night and listening to the station, the disc jockey started to say that "I got a request here from 'Good old England' for a song to be played for his American friend." He then went on to say that this request had come from – and there was a rather awkward pause before he stammered out that the request had been sent from – "Glow Sester, in Glow Sester Shire." I could not contain my amusement and was still laughing when a couple of the other Middies returned from the shore after a night at the pictures. In disbelief they questioned the pronunciation of Gloucester and Gloucestershire, but literally as we were talking about it, unbelievably there came another request from "Good Old England – this time from Whor Sester in Whor Sester Shire."

You couldn't make it up!

We sailed from New York a couple of days later, and no-one thought to retune the radio to its short-wave band so we could listen to transmissions from the BBC World Service. On about the second day out from the American coast, we turned the radio back on and were amazed to hear WINS still booming through loud and clear. Preferring this to the rather staid BBC, we left it alone and continued to listen. Don McReary explained that he was absolutely amazed as he knew from experience that you couldn't receive WINS in New York State a couple of miles clear of the New York city limits so how we were continuing to get the station so far out into the Atlantic was a complete mystery!

On that fateful day, 22nd November, 1963, while listening to WINS on that Pye Cambridge radio in our cabin far out into the Atlantic, we heard of the dreadful assassination of President Kennedy. It stunned us all and there was some acute sadness among the crew of the ship, as we all considered ourselves 'adopted' Americans seeing that we traded between the far-flung ports of the Far East and the Good Old 'U S of A'.

Teucer, one of the three 'Silver Line' ships acquired by Blue Funnel, sister ship to the *Telamon* on which I served for my round the world trip in 114 days.

Trespassers Will be Prosecuted

One of the most difficult things we had to learn when we started our training on the SR.N6 hovercraft was getting used to handling the engine. The fine control of the delicate relationship between engine power, propellor pitch and lift fan speed was crucial to many of the manoeuvres we carried out while flying the beasts and, coupled with the restrictions on accelerating and decelerating the engines without causing them to cut out, a great amount of practice was needed until we got this balance right.

The training period in an empty craft was probably the best fun time that we had throughout our careers in the hovercraft industry as we had sole use of one of these beasts, no passengers of course, and just about the whole of the Solent to 'play in'. In order to give us the opportunity to perfect this delicate balance of propellor pitch, lift fan speed and engine power, we used to practise some exercises in odd spots so that we did not endanger anyone else while we were 'playing',

One such spot was a long straight stretch of beach at the seaward end of Southampton Water between the entrance to the Hamble River and Hillhead Point on the Hampshire coast. This beach, accessible from the sea only over mud flats, was ideal as it had a reasonably sloped sand and shingle embankment which we would approach over the mud flats, climb the slope and sit the craft down, hopefully without sliding backwards. Once we had perfected this, we would then try to lift the craft back on to the 'hover' and, using the power of the engine and a balanced amount of propellor pitch, hold the craft stationary on this slope, before angling the craft slightly one way or the other, and making the craft slide bodily sideways, travelling along the sloping beach without falling backwards onto the mud flats. Once we got it right, there was a great feeling of being completely in control, and it honed our handling skills and gave us confidence. Our Senior Commander, Adrian, who undertook our training was pretty relaxed once he had got us through this initial training exercise, and could then continue onto other aspects of our intensive training before we were let loose carrying passengers.

On this particular occasion the other two trainees, Ken and John, with whom I was undergoing training had completed their turns 'in the seat' and it was my turn to have a go. Taking over on the slope we turned and headed back out to sea to return to the beach for this short, steep beach landing which I executed with moderate success, and I prepared to start my sideways slide across the line of the beach. With it being dead low water, coming in to land from over the water across the mud flats meant that the windows of the craft were somewhat spattered with mud, and I washed the front cockpit windows off with the wipers and washers. Shutting the small sliding side window alongside the Commander's seat, I gingerly picked the craft up once more, got the balance just about right and set off sideways, picking up speed to about 15 knots.

I think everyone knows about premonitions and the feeling of the hairs on the back of one's neck bristling. Well for some reason I decided to open the small sliding window panel set into the large, fixed side window alongside my seat. This gave me a perfect view through the mud-spattered large side window of a gentleman walking his dog along the beach who, on seeing this 12-ton hovercraft hurtling sideways towards him at speed, had frozen in his footsteps. I immediately reacted and by going into reverse pitch on the propellor spun the craft round and headed back onto the water. Adrian yelled at me and asked what I thought I was doing until, as we turned, he also saw the shocked face of this poor chap through the clean front windows as we swung very rapidly round and slid straight back onto the mud flats. After regaining our composure, it was thought that the best thing to do was to go back and apologise to this poor unfortunate chap whose morning dog walk had been so rudely interrupted by these mad clowns in their hovercraft.

Turning round again, I approached the beach slowly to land once more near to this gentleman, but in vain. He saw us approaching again, decided we were coming to have another go and dropped his dog's lead and simply ran for cover, with us not exactly chasing him but trying to follow him in order to offer our apologies. In the end Adrian told me to sit the craft down, shut down the engine, and we would approach him on foot and proffer our apologies. This eventually happened, and a rather embarrassing interview ensued, with the gentleman telling us exactly where we could put our hovercraft, with or without its engine running.

Another place we used to practise this short steep beach landing was the shingle beach in Osborne Bay on the island. This beach was somewhat more difficult to land on properly as it was a lot steeper than the Hillhead Beach, there were no mud flats over which to travel before hitting the bottom of the beach and there was only just enough beach to accommodate the length of the SR.N6.

Osborne Bay beach is now open and visited by the general public after English Heritage took over the running of Osborne House in the 1980s. It is of great historical significance as Queen Victoria and Prince Albert's holiday home on the island and she used the beach to swim in the

Solent when she holidayed there. The bathing machines that she used are now a major attraction on that beautifully restored beach area. After Prince Albert died, she used Osborne House as a reclusive retreat to mourn the loss of her husband, and it became a virtual no-go area for the local population for many years. After her death in 1901, Edward VII gifted the house to the nation and it served as a Royal Naval Training College for many years. I remember that when we lived on the island it was only possible to visit the royal apartments in an organised group and the grounds were not available for walking in. Indeed, the area immediately behind the beach in the bay was totally overgrown with bramble bushes and there were large trees pretty much right down to the shoreline. This of course made the beach an attractive spot for us to practise; at least there should be no dog walkers!

Practising on this beach a few days after the dog walker incident at Hillhead, John and I had completed our turns at attempting this rather more difficult landing with mixed success. Getting the final approach speed before hitting the base of the slope was the key, and poor Adrian was getting a little flustered – firstly I was too slow, then too fast, John had suffered similar criticisms and we were both a little disheartened at not being able to get it right. Vacating the seat so Ken could have his turn, John and I retreated to the rear of the craft to sit and chat about our shortcomings and watch Ken from a distance making a similarly tentative approach while being yelled at by Adrian that he was too slow. Turning the craft around at the foot of the beach, Ken proceeded back out into the bay, turned and made another approach. John and I were deep in conversation as we approached yet again, until John suddenly stopped talking and said to me, "Blimey, isn't Ken just a little fast this time?" We both froze. Adrian, whose attention had been diverted by something else, suddenly realised that Ken was indeed a little rapid and we mounted the bottom of the slope, careered up to the crest of the beach and over the top of the embankment into the brambles and undergrowth on the shore.

By this time Ken had reacted and had shut the throttle of the engine to bring the craft to a halt, slithering through the jungle of plants, nettles and brambles, and coming to a halt in front of a tree on which was fastened a sign in large red letters:

Osborne House – Private Property
Keep Out
Trespassers Will Be Prosecuted

We all sat in silence for a few moments, wondering what Adrian was going to say, but we needn't have worried. Being no fool, Adrian simply asked Ken to vacate the seat, jumped into it himself and instructed the three of us to hop off the craft and help to push the bow round and assist him to manoeuvre back out of the jungle and onto the beach, before re-boarding the three of us and returning to Cowes for a coffee break.

Returning home that evening after training for the day was over, my wife asked what on earth I had been doing as I was scratched to death by the brambles, and my clothes stained from the greenery that comprised the undergrowth. Indeed, on entering the terminal at Cowes for our coffee break there were a few raised eyebrows and wry comments such as, "Been gardening, have we?"

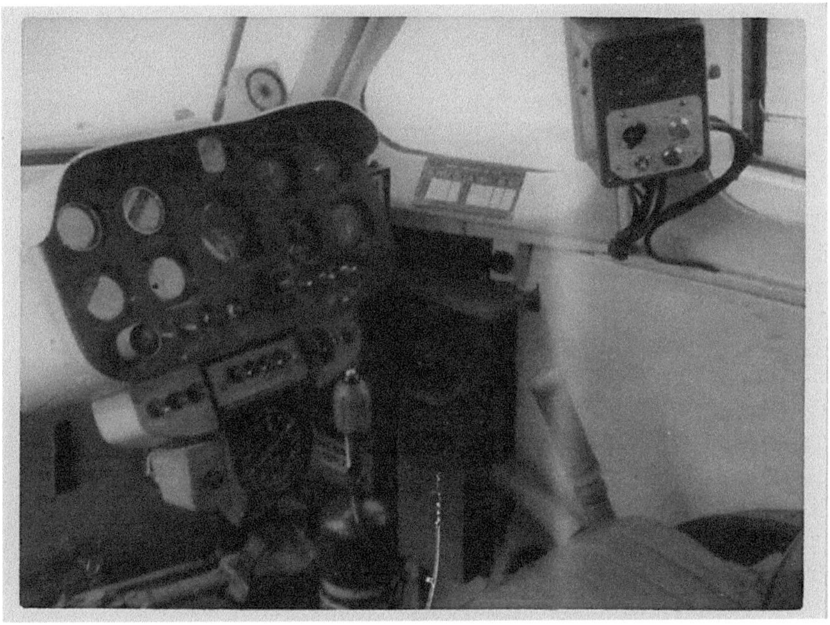

Controls of an SR.N6 hovercraft.

Two Wheels on my Wagon?

When coming ashore after completing the required time at sea to allow me to sit my various certificates of competency, transport was always a question that had to be addressed. Completing my time as an indentured Midshipman early in 1965, I was not exactly flush with ready cash, and in order to travel from my parents' home on the outskirts of Hull to the college in the city, I purchased a second-hand James motorbike from one of the second-hand bike shops near to the college, for the princely sum of £8. Flash it was not! But it was relatively reliable and got me to the college every day for the four weeks I spent studying, although I did leave it behind on examination days to travel by bus into Hull as I didn't want to miss the actual exams through an unplanned breakdown. When I had finished and passed my Second Mates Foreign Going Certificate, the first of my professional sets of exams, the motorbike was sold for £10, thus I was £2 up. That motorbike I had for Second Mates was an incredibly cheap way to provide myself with transport, and I repeated the process when, 18 months later, I came ashore again to study and sit for my First Mates Foreign Going Certificate.

This time I really splashed out, and spent £10 on an Ambassador motorbike, which was a very reliable bike again, with one small quirk. I remember the first day I attended at the college and opened my case with all my books and navigational equipment in it. The chap with whom I shared a desk asked me why on earth I had a plug spanner in amongst all my books and other necessary navigation equipment? I simply said that if he wanted to watch me at the end of the school day, he would see why. That bike simply would not start on the kick starter unless you took the plug out, blew across it once, re-inserted it into the top of the cylinder, and kicked the engine over again. Then it would start first time, but unless you went through that procedure every time, you could pump the starter until you were blue in the face. That bike saw me through with ease the six weeks I was ashore, and I sold it on again for £12 to another student who was behind me on the course – and I threw in the plug spanner for free!

During all that time, what I really wanted was the most reliable motorbike of the day, a BSA Bantam, British made by the Birmingham Small Arms Company in the Midlands of England, and it had a reliability record stretching back over a couple of decades. I could never afford one when I was in the lower ranks, but when I was about to come ashore in 1970 to take my Masters Foreign Going Certificate exams, I was a little more solvent. I was married by that time and living in Portsmouth, my new wife had a good teaching job in Purbrook on the outskirts of the city, and we had a car. However, she needed the car to get to work every day, and I had to travel the 20 or so miles to the College of Navigation at Warsash on the River Hamble. So I took the plunge and bought a second-hand BSA Bantam with the new 175cc engine fitted to it, as the Japanese bike market was starting to overtake and make the British designs of the time redundant and outdated. I bought the bike in the autumn of 1970 before I actually came ashore and used it to travel the 75 miles up to London to join one of the last ships I served on, taking it on board with me for the duration of the 'coasting' voyage. Sadly, mechanically, it was not all roses with that bike, and when I finally left the ship one evening at about 2000 to travel home after being relieved, the weather was not very nice. A typical grey December day had turned to rain and it was cold. I dressed appropriately for the trip down the A3 (it would be years before the M3 was completed) and off I went.

The first breakdown occurred after about five miles, and I managed to fix it after a while with my basic tool kit that I carried on board and set off again. Travelling around the Kingston upon Thames by-pass, the bike came to an ominous stop once more, and I wheeled it into a layby to examine the problem. By now the rain was coming down in 'stair rods', and I struggled for about an hour without success to fix an electrical problem that seemed to bug the machine. At about half past ten, a Ford Transit panel van pulled up alongside me in the layby, emblazoned with the title 'Clarks Racing Team of Kingston' plastered all across the rear side panels, and a chap got out to ask if he could help. Taking a look, he said, "Come on chum, you'll not fix it in this weather," and he and another chap helped me to load it into the back of their van, and off we went. They had apparently seen me about half an hour previously and wondered what I was up to, but were on a business trip so couldn't stop. They went past me again and then doubled back to see if they could offer help. This I gratefully accepted, as being a simple sailor I was totally at a loss as to how to fix this problem. On arrival at their garage, I was welcomed by the two lads' respective girlfriends who proceeded to warm me up with a hot drink and a Pot Noodle and placed me in front of their fire while the two mechanics stripped the electrical system down and fixed the problem. I was so incredibly grateful, and they had chatted to me about life in general and enquired why I was travelling so late at night. I explained and they asked me where I was bound, expressing some disbelief when I said 'Portsmouth'.

The weather had deteriorated even more, with a light dusting of snow now descending, but I was determined to get home as I hadn't seen my wife for nearly two months, and Christmas was looming – our first together ashore and at home for nearly two years. So I set off again after donning my wet weather gear, which consisted of a bright yellow fisherman's smock which my wife had shortened for me so I could sit on the bike comfortably, and a pair of heavy duty black waterproof trousers to keep my lower half dry. I had also purchased a pair of RAF flying boots to ride the bike, and to complete the ensemble I wore my wife's former college scarf wrapped around the lower part of my face so that only my eyes were visible, and topped the lot off with my motorcycle crash helmet. I must have looked like a south cardinal light buoy with all that lot on – yellow over black being the south indicator in the new cardinal buoyage system! Thanking these garage Samaritans with all my heart and soul for looking after me, and wishing them and their lovely girlfriends a Happy Christmas, I set off once more to travel the next 60-odd miles home.

I had the A3 almost to myself that night, as I was the only idiot still out and about, and the other concern that now presented itself was petrol for the fuel tank. Getting fuel was a problem in the dark nights of those days as most garages shut up shop at about 10pm, and the only petrol station that showed any signs of life on that trip was on the outskirts of Guildford, where a 'Money in the Slot' forecourt pump was lit up. Unfortunately, I didn't have any of the correct coins to put into the slot, so I had to soldier on and hope for the best. On reaching the top of Portsdown Hill on the outskirts of Portsmouth and seeing the twinkling lights of my new adopted city stretched out below me, I actually ran out of fuel.

Knowing there was an all-night garage on the A27 which crossed the A3 at the bottom of the hill, I coasted down powerless and freewheeled onto the forecourt, stopping alongside a petrol pump. I pressed the button to enliven the pump, but the lady on the till was deep in conversation with a girlfriend and her boyfriend in the kiosk and didn't notice me at the pump. So I went to the window and tapped on it. I must have made a pretty sight, as on turning around the girl and her lady friend screamed with fright at this apparition staring at them through the kiosk window, and I must have given them a real shock. After filling up, I went to the window to pay for the petrol and apologised for frightening them. They had actually recovered by that time, and she explained that her two friends had been to see a scary sci-fi film at the cinema that previous evening and had called in to the garage to tell the lady cashier all about it!

I kept that troublesome BSA motorbike for the 10-week duration of my study at Warsash and then traded it in for a 50cc Honda moped which I used while working in Portsmouth for SeaSpeed and then for several years without any problems whilst we lived on the Isle of Wight. When we eventually moved house from Portsmouth to the island I asked the senior Solent Commander, Adrian, if I could stick my little lightweight moped on the stern of the HM2 Hovercraft, to save myself the cost on the car ferry. I could not believe what Adrian said to me in reply. He considered it to be a severe fire risk, and if I wanted to take it on the hovercraft, I would have to drain the fuel tank and fill it with sugar to eradicate the risk. Everyone else couldn't believe what he had said either, and I'm afraid I merely waited until he wasn't about and took it across anyway!

But the one Portsmouth motoring 'incident' that I will

never forget was when I was home on leave while still at sea, in between voyages to the Far East. In those days during the 1960s, there wasn't a lot of cash floating about, the country's economic recovery had not really hit its target, and people took whatever cheap alternatives of transport they could find. One of these 'cheap and cheerful' options was the Bond three-wheeled car, accessible to a lot of people as they were cheap to buy, very economical to run, one only needed a motor cycle licence to drive them, and they were peanuts to insure. Fitted with a tiny 247cc air-cooled two-stroke motorbike engine they were rugged little workhorses and provided an affordable alternative to the more expensive Mini that was taking the country by storm. Initially built of aluminium, they were one of the first cars to have fibreglass bodywork. They of course had their own intrinsic problems and quirks. Having two wheels at the rear and one in the front, they were somewhat unstable, but if driven carefully they would get you from A to B in basic comfort in the dry; not very quickly with their small, air-cooled motorbike engines balanced over and driving the single front wheel, but they got you there.

Trying to corner at speed was fraught with danger, and this was demonstrated to me one day when I was out and about driving in the city and came to a T-junction with a main road. About 200 yards to the right of this junction, where I was patiently waiting to access the main road was a sharp bend, and I saw a Bond three-wheel car negotiating this bend at speed, the rear wheel on the inside of the turn lifting off the road as it cornered. It dropped back on to its three wheels once around the bend, but at the very last moment the driver indicated to turn left into the road that I was waiting in, didn't noticeably reduce his speed at all, and as he took the sharp turn into the road, the whole thing tipped on to its right-hand side, and slithered to a halt right alongside my car waiting at the junction.

I sat in the driving seat of my car looking at the roof of this Bond car now on its side extremely close to the side of my car. Wondering what would happen next, I noticed that the plucky little engine was still running. Not knowing what to do, I simply sat there somewhat stunned, and then the passenger side door of this little car which was now pointing toward the heavens was flung open by its driver who clambered up and out of the car on to the road. Squeezing in between the side of my car and the roof of his vehicle, he simply pushed the thing back on to its three wheels, wrenched the driver's side door open, and clambered back in. The whole side of the fibreglass body of the car was scratched and cracked but he didn't seem at all concerned. Realising I was in very close proximity to him and his car and mouth wide open in wonderment, he muttered to me in an irritated and somewhat embarrassed voice, "Bloody thing is always doing this!" and promptly drove off.

It then dawned upon me that I must be holding up traffic

behind me, and on glancing in the rear-view mirror of my car I observed the chap in the car next in the queue with this head on the steering wheel in absolute fits of laughter, with tears running down his cheeks! Eventually gathering ourselves together we negotiated the exit from the junction and carried on our way still laughing and remembering the total indifference of this mad three-wheel car driver!

All Creatures Great and Small

Throughout my life I have had a great affinity with animals, and working at sea did not diminish this affection for everything four legged. While working at sea with the Blue Funnel Line, we carried many different animals on the ships, mainly dogs as passengers that belonged to service personnel and their entire families stationed in the Far East, and which were transported back to the UK on our ships ahead of their owners' return. In the days of rabies being rife all over the world except thankfully not in the UK, these poor animals were subjected to a long period of quarantine when they arrived in England and their owners could visit their dogs whilst they were locked up and frequently tested to ensure they had not brought this dreaded fatal disease into the country.

My own personal ownership of dogs started before our son was born in 1972; we bought a lovely black Labrador puppy on the Isle of Wight a few months before our son's birth in order to get all the puddles and piles out of the way in advance of Alastair's arrival, but it proved unnecessary as that dog seemed to be born house trained! So, our son and later our daughter were brought up with animals right from the start, and they both now have dogs of their own. We progressed through that lovely Labrador to a scatty English Setter, and then three successive Flat Coat Retrievers, the last of which is beside me now as I write.

Other animals that we carried at sea varied enormously from pedigree pigs to China for breeding purposes, race horses between ports in the Far East for attending various race meetings in different countries, to a full circus from

Australia to Singapore on one of the ships that served that route. I understood from a colleague that was on the ship at the time that the crew were overwhelmed by the presence of those exotic breeds which varied from tigers in cages via giraffes in the holds (with the hatch coverings left off for air) to some friendly elephants that eventually had to be intermittently shackled and chained to strong points on the deck of the ship to avoid the ship taking on a list when they decided to wander around the deck and all congregate on one side or the other!

As Midshipmen we were usually allocated the care of these lovely additions to the passenger list, and I looked after quite a few dogs as well as pigs and a couple of cats. An additional lure towards taking on the care of these animals was that we were awarded a cash bonus, something that certainly was welcome as my monthly salary when I first commenced my apprenticeship was £6 a month! There were, however, some people who always thought they were the only ones who could look after the more valuable animals, and one rather unpopular Chief Officer I sailed with took on the role of looking after one of the racehorses we carried from Singapore up to Bangkok, thus denying the Midshipmen the cash they would have earned. This particular horse was a bad-tempered animal that everyone used to avoid – usually everyone would stop by and talk to the animals, even the pigs, that were housed in proper stalls on the deck of the ship. But this Chief Officer was convinced he was the only one to be competent enough to care for this horse, until one day it bit him and he had to attend the sick bay for the male nurse to dress his wounds. That caused some wry smiles from the rest of the ship's company, and when he still tried to claim the money for looking after the horse, there was something of a revolt and general condemnation of his selfish attitude.

When I became a Pilot on the Humber, it was not uncommon to find animals on the small ships that traded to the river. There were quite a lot of Master/owners among the Dutch and German ships that frequented the ports on the estuary, and sometimes these ships were also their family homes. Children would be born and brought up aboard these floating houses, and pets were commonplace as in similar shoreside situations. Dogs abounded, cats were also common and there were even the occasional exotic birds in cages. As a dog owner I usually had a couple of treats in my coat pocket, and these proved useful in getting to know these animals that roamed pretty freely around the wheelhouses of the ships, sharing the space with playpens for the small children. However, some encounters were not quite so pleasant and stick in my mind...

In the wee small hours of one morning, I was given the job of taking a small German coaster away from the Old Harbour in Hull, which had travelled down from a berth further up the River Hull on the previous tide, but the Master had asked for an overnight layby berth to delay his departure in order to get some rest for himself and his crew before going out to sea. The ship was tied up alongside a couple of barges, and after carefully clambering over these barges in the darkness of the night, I swung my leg over the rail of this coaster in order to get aboard, to be met by a row of white teeth and the baying sound of a large and somewhat unfriendly German Shepherd dog. Making a hasty retreat I stood on the barge while this rather large beast bayed at me, and deciding that discretion was the better part of valour, I returned to the Harbour Master's office nearby.

Explaining to the Harbour Master that I couldn't get

aboard because of this dog, he said that he had warned the Master not to let this beast roam loose, as quarantine regulations at the time had been tightened due to a possibility of the invasion of rabies into the country and were very strict, so consequently the Port Health Authorities had forbidden dogs to be allowed to roam loose while the ships were in port. Calling the ship on the VHF radio from the Harbour Master's office elicited no reply at all, so I proceeded back to the ship to attempt to get aboard once more. Picking up a large heavy shackle from the deck of the adjacent barge I hammered on the side of the ship to try to rouse someone in the crew, but all to no avail. The time came eventually when there wasn't enough time to get the ship out to sea as it was well past high water, so I returned to the Pilot Office to explain why I had had to cancel the ship. As I entered the office, the Master of the ship in question called and demanded to know where his Pilot was, only to be told in no uncertain terms that if he wanted a Pilot to board his ship, he should not leave an unattended and vicious dog roaming loose around the decks, and that his Pilot – me – had been trying to get aboard for the last two hours! Port Health Officials apparently went to see the Master later in the day, and he was let off the fine that could have been applied as the dog hadn't actually managed to get hold of me and bite me!

Very early on in my career, just after I had become a Humber Pilot, one of my first jobs was a small Dutch vessel called the *Triumph*, one of Mr. 'Becks' of Groningen. She was bound for Grimsby Docks and, being small and comparatively light drafted, I entered the lock at Grimsby from the river at about two and a half hours to high water. The wing of the ship's bridge was level with the dock wall, and as we settled in the lock, I asked the Dock Master which berth the ship was for in the dock system. He gaily replied, "Nickersons," and walked back into his office on the lock.

The Master of the ship, a very pleasant elderly Dutchman, said to me that he hadn't been there for years, and I replied that I had better go ashore into the Dock Master's office to check the latest soundings in the dock to make sure we wouldn't ground on the way to the berth. During our training on the river before being licenced, we had to accompany Pilots to as many of the dozens of berths situated throughout the district as we could, providing of course there were ships bound for those berths. Entering the Dock Master's office, I merely asked him, "Where the ruddy hell is Nickersons?"

That brought a huge smile to the Dock Master's face, and he showed me on the chart where it was, tucked away in the far corner of a basically disused corner of Union Dock – a dock which is now inaccessible as a major new road bridge has been built over its entrance to take the new and much improved A180 across it towards Cleethorpes.

Returning to the ship we left the lock, now level with the water inside the dock, and proceeded to the difficult right-angled turn into Union Dock. This dock had mainly been given over to private moorings for motor boats, and had vertical piles driven into the bed of the dock to permit these boats to tie up to, making the passage through to Nickersons Flour Mill difficult to say the least. Add to that the fact that it was the middle of the night, we proceeded very slowly and cautiously to the berth, weaving our way through these piles and boats moored to them with the help of a very powerful searchlight that was thankfully fitted to the ship. After we had reached the berth, we realised that there were no boatmen to tie the ship up on the quay, but the resourceful crew of the ship jumped ashore once we had put the bows on to the quay and tied up in a short space of time.

Thanking me for careful and successful job, the Master then invited me down for a beer before I left the ship, and we chatted about the failing trade of the carrying of corn and other grains direct to installations such as Nickersons for processing, the majority of the transport at that time being transferred to road haulage and the small ships losing yet another trade route.

I left the ship after about 20 minutes to walk back to the lock head and our Pilot's lobby on the dock. Reaching the gates of the compound I found them locked and barred and I was unable to climb the gates as there was some vicious-looking barbed wire atop the gates to deter any unwanted guests. So I decided to walk back through the compound and call the dock and the Pilot station at Spurn to ask for someone to come and let me out, and that was when I came across the problem. It was a repeat of the Old Harbour saga, but this time there were two of these lovable German Shepherd dogs on the loose, and they corralled me in a rather dark corner for some time. Lost for what to do, I stayed until they lost interest, and I managed to hightail it to back to the ship for refuge. On re-boarding the ship, I explained to the Master and crew who were very sympathetic, and we called the dock and the Pilot station to try to resolve the problem. As it happened, the Pilot Master had despatched a Pilot launch from Spurn to collect some Grimsby-based Pilots to take them to the Spurn Point sea station for boarding ships, so he merely sent the launch into the dock to find me. I had to guide the launch to the berth as the coxswain had no clue where the berth was either, and he eventually found me and I left the ship via the launch and was taken back to Spurn as the easiest way to get back to the Pilot Office and my car in Hull!

It turned out later that the ship apparently wasn't expected on that particular tide, and the compound and facility had been left in the charge of the two four-legged guards, and was also the reason why there were no boatmen to take the ship's ropes when we arrived at the quay!

That was one occasion where my affinity to dogs didn't quite work!

Skipper, our second Flat Coat Retriever.

Island Characters

Life on the Isle of Wight was, for my wife and I, a whole new revelation. Whilst I was working the Portsmouth to Ryde route flying the HM2 craft, we were required to reside in Portsmouth near to the base where the HM2 craft were berthed overnight. On being selected for further training and permanent employment in SeaSpeed, we needed to move to the island near to or actually in West Cowes. As we already lived in a rented flat in Portsmouth where my wife had a good teaching job, the first bit was easy, and we started house hunting immediately my new permanent post was confirmed, eventually finding our first home in West Cowes, about five minutes' drive from the terminal.

While flying the HM2s, we had a crew of two – myself as Commander and a Coxswain, who made the ropes fast on the berth when we arrived, generally assisted with the passengers, but most importantly was there to steer the craft in foggy conditions while the Commander peered into the radar and guided the craft across the Solent from berth to berth. We had some really nice chaps to work with, some who were recruited in for the summer seasons when we ran two HM2s in opposition, and some who were from the permanent staff strength resident on the island. Ted Andrews, a Northern Irishman, was a former Royal Naval Marine who had served in the 2nd World War, and he and I had an immediate affinity as I learned that he had landed in North Africa from the *Glenearn*, one of the Glen Line ships I had sailed on as a Midshipman during my time at sea. She had been requisitioned by the Royal Navy during the war as a troop landing ship and served in the Mediterranean and on the D-Day landings, and had carried

Ted and his mates into the beaches for the landings in North Africa. The other Coxswain, Brian Ireland, was a true islander, a born and bred 'Caulk Head' as they were known from the islanders' adeptness at caulking the ships of the Navy during Nelson's day, that painstaking task of introducing and hammering in a seal of oakum between the planks of ships to make them watertight.

Brian used to regale us with myths and stories about 'island life' and we enjoyed a playful and happy banter during those hard-working days flashing back and forth between the island and the mainland. Certain things stick in my mind, one of which was that Brian reckoned it would only take us three months before we became 'island minded', that wonderful state of mind where 'tomorrow will do'.

I'm afraid I didn't believe this as I pronounced that I was a mainlander and wouldn't fall into the trap of being so lazy. Shortly after we moved in and settled into our house in Cowes, there was a need for me to go to Newport, some four miles away, in the car to collect some groceries from the cash and carry that couldn't be obtained in Cowes. We had lived in Cowes for about five weeks after moving from Portsmouth, and I'm afraid that we had fallen right into the trap. I said to my wife that I couldn't be bothered to go that day but would go tomorrow – the 'mañana' syndrome had struck. Then we brought each other up with a 'round turn' and laughed that it had only taken us a few weeks, not months, to fall into the trap. Our life on the island was idyllic, we had four happy years there and met some wonderful people. Our two children were born there and gave us some real joy and pleasure, as they do to this day.

But most of all our time there introduced us to some wonderful friends and colleagues, all of them characters in their own right and who provided us with a lot of laughs. In our sister company, Hovertravel, who operated from Ryde to Southsea, they mainly employed former 'flyers' – helicopter pilots, light aircraft drivers, and those who had trained to fly aircraft of one sort or another. One of these gentlemen was a former wartime RAF Pilot, George Blackburn, who as a young man had flown Lancaster bombers during the war, and he used to tell of having to put his left boot (or was it his right boot? I can never remember!) hard down immediately after take-off to counteract the swing generated by the propellors on the Lancaster all rotating the same way, thus causing the plane to slew wildly away from the direction of travel. He used to laugh it all off, and I can imagine, though will never know, the incredible strain those men were under during those dark days of the 1940s. He again used to laugh it all off by wearing white kid leather gauntlets to drive the SR.N6 on its route, one with an 'L' on it and the other with an 'R' on it, just to lighten the days. When asked, "How are you today, George?" his reply in his somewhat out of place broad Lancashire accent was always the same: "Struggling on for a crust Old Boy."

In SeaSpeed we had our own ex-war veteran as well. John Bishop had flown as a Navigator in the Swordfish aircraft that had attacked and damaged the *Bismarck* in the early part of the war, succeeding in slowing her down for the home fleet to catch and attack her. He used to regale us of stories of having to lash the Swordfish planes down to the deck of the carriers, otherwise with their immense 'lift' from their biplane wing arrangement, they could lift off all on their own, crewless, from the deck of the carrier when she was steaming at full speed into a stiff wind. He also used to tell us of watching the carrier steam away from under them as they took off from the flight deck on a sortie, a testament to the air capabilities and design of that fine old machine that the German guns couldn't hit as they flew too slowly. The gun sights on the enemy ships were set for a minimum flying speed of 100 knots, the Swordfish was lucky to be able to reach 70 knots, thus the German bullets went over or underneath them!

We also had the slightly eccentric members of the team, one of whom was one of the original navigators for the SR.N4 at Dover when that service started, and who had reluctantly succumbed to training on the SR.N6 in Cowes in order to keep pace financially with the 'new-start' Commanders who came to the job after him. An accurate log of engine hours had to be kept when flying the gas turbine powered craft, the SR.N6 and SR.N4, and for that an accurate timepiece was needed. Whereas all the Commanders in Cowes owned and used reliable wristwatches for this purpose, Paul from Dover decided that he would use his bedside travelling alarm clock. What impression that gave to passengers boarding and walking past Paul sitting in the seat with an alarm clock beside him on a little shelf I cannot imagine. Possibly that he would have set the alarm to wake him up before arriving at Southampton? Who knows!

He did on one occasion come to Cowes to help out on the roster while we were training and was subsequently delegated to carry out one short session of our training while the Senior Commander, Adrian, was called away for a meeting. That proved fun as he never really took to flying the SR.N6 craft and was never comfortable with it, whereas he was totally at home on the flight deck of the SR.N4 out of sight of passengers while navigating the mighty SR.N4 across the channel. Therefore, we didn't really learn much that morning except how not to handle the throttle of the Gnome gas turbine engine. If you were too violent with it, the engine would cut out on you either from too rapid acceleration or deceleration, the former causing an over rapid rise in temperature in the combustion chamber of the engine, and the latter causing a breakdown of the flow of air vital to the operation of any gas turbine.

But one of the funniest things that I heard was from the Harbour Master of Cowes. Henry Wright was a good friend to us all in SeaSpeed and travelled on the craft regularly. He would always sit in the front seat and chat to us, and we would discuss anything and everything from cricket to how busy he was organising the yachting and sailing fraternity in the Mecca of sailing, Cowes. During the summer period, the Harbour Masters of the differing places on the island, Yarmouth, Bembridge, Newtown, Ryde and of course Cowes, would gather together weekly to discuss how busy they were, how many berths they had available, and how the season was progressing. These meetings were held and hosted alternately by the different Harbour Masters, and it was after one of these occasions when Henry boarded the craft to travel to Southampton with a large grin still showing on his face. After lifting off and clearing the harbour at Cowes, I asked Henry what was tickling him. He seemed reluctant at first to relate the story but did so after I pressed him.

They had all just met at Yarmouth, where in those days there were mainly just floating moorings at buoys in the confines of the harbour for yachts to tie up to. Apparently, the Yarmouth Harbour Master had received a request from a gentleman from Birmingham for a mooring for his new 18' 6" yacht that was on a trailer at his home in the Midlands. Having been allocated a berth, the gentleman had then driven his car towing this new boat on its trailer down to Lymington, and crossed on the car ferry to Yarmouth, complete with boat still on trailer. Once there he launched his boat from the trailer into the water and motored it to his new berth. Coming back ashore, he then re-boarded the ferry with his now empty trailer behind his car and returned home to Birmingham. The following weekend, keen to go sailing, he had driven back to Lymington, boarded the ferry and travelled to Yarmouth once more to board his boat and spend the weekend pottering about on the water. However, on boarding his boat at its mooring, he noticed some rainwater that had collected in the cockpit, and in order to drain this water out, had drilled a hole in the bottom of the boat to let it out...

Henry couldn't help laughing out loud again as he related this story, and I tackled him and accused him of making it all up. He was absolutely adamant, the Yarmouth Harbour Master had shown all the other Harbour Masters the tip of the yacht's mast still sticking out above the water at its mooring, and they had all stared incredulously at the sight. Divers were summoned to assess the situation, and had promised to return as soon as they could to salvage and re-float the yacht with air bags.

I have to admit that I couldn't take this on board, and after I had finished my session of duty that morning, I drove to Yarmouth to have a look for myself. There it was, all true, no 'wind-up' – a sad and rather pathetic sight!

Surely, you're not Taking me in There, Mr Pilot?

At the entrance to the River Hull there now stands an amphitheatre called the Stage@TheDock, created from what was originally a dry dock called Central Dry Dock or Southend Graving Dock, first built in 1843. This dry dock had quite a history and was closed for many years in the late 1960s and early 1970s due to union dominance, the owners not being able to make a go of it.

However, in the 1970s when the Drypool Dry Dock and Engineering Company closed its workshop doors for the last time, their well-regarded and respected foreman/manager Len Laithwaite saw an opportunity to make a new career both for himself and many of his former workmates who had been made redundant. What Len didn't know about shipbuilding and ship repairing wasn't worth knowing and could be written on the back of a postage stamp. His knowledge and skills were well known, and he seized the opportunity to carve out a new era for that rather sad looking and neglected dry dock at the mouth of the River Hull. He quite simply bought the dry dock, lock, stock and barrel.

Len started recruiting from the local area, and one of his strict conditions was that there was to be no union involvement or activity in the yard. The brother-in-law of one of our launch crew was a time-served experienced welder who went for a job there. At his interview he was told in no uncertain terms that if he wanted the job as a welder, when there was welding to be done, he would do it. However, when there was no welding to be done, he would have to be prepared to undertake other menial tasks in and around the yard such as sweeping up, painting etc. Initially the applicant took this as an affront, but then realised that in those times when jobs were scarce and hard to find, he would 'give it a go' and see how he got on. He openly admitted that after a few months working for Len, the work was so abundant that it was the best move he had ever made and his future was, at the time, secure.

Indeed, the reputation of the yard's efficiency and standard of work spread and became well known for the speed at which it was carried out together with the skills that were employed and utilised, and its fame spread. The ship repair yards on the continent were very efficient, and the practices were far superior to that of the usual British equivalent yards, but Len sought to equal that reputation, and in fact succeeded in bettering the efficiency and speed at which ships could be repaired and put back out into service after suffering damage. A ship that is in a dry dock undergoing repairs is not earning any money for its owners.

One such ship was a small German coaster that had suffered some damage whilst loading scrap metal at a South Wales river berth, the scrap being bound for Portugal. The range of the rise and fall of the tide on the Bristol Channel is well known and is large; a tidal range from high to low water of 10 metres is usual, with tides in excess of 13 metres being not uncommon. The ship had been loading on one of the numerous river berths, and whilst swinging the scrap across from wharf to ship in a grab attached to a crane, some of the scrap had fallen out of the grab and ended up on the bottom of the river between ship and wharf. When the tide had fallen and the ship sat on the bottom to 'dry out', being left high and dry on the mud, a sharp piece of the scrap had punctured the ship's hull at the 'turn of the bilge', the point where the vertical ship's side is curved and then meets the horizontal ship's bottom. Fortunately, this incursion into the ship's hull was in one of the wing ballast tanks, and no water actually entered into the ship's hatch.

The Master had summoned the surveyor from Germanischer Lloyd, the Hamburg based ship classification society (similar to Lloyds of London) who were responsible to the ship's insurers for looking after the safety of the ship at sea. After discussion and examination of the damage a plan was hatched so that the ship could go to Portugal, offload the scrap metal, and then re-load a cargo of box timber (a low-grade wood used for making cases and pallets) and return to the River Trent to discharge. The one condition was that she would then have to be dry docked and repaired on the Humber before being allowed to return to sea and continue trading. This was in the early days of the resurrected Central Dry Dock, now known as Ruscadors Ship Repair and Dry Dock Company, and the reputation of the yard was just beginning to be established. Thus, the dry docking was fixed and that was when, early one morning, I was allocated to the job of taking her into the dry dock from the Hull Roads anchorage, where she had been parked after coming down from the River Trent on the previous tide.

I was, however, ordered to be on board far too early; the time for entering the dry dock was at about 30 minutes to high water, and I was ordered to be on board at two and a half hours to high water – a mistake – but the golden rule of the Pilot service was: 'You must attend at the time allotted'. So I proceeded to board the ship where it was anchored, to be met by a rather disgruntled and surly German Captain who didn't seem at all pleased to be going into this 'Mickey Mouse' dry dock and he was even less pleased to be told that

I was far too early and we wouldn't be going anywhere for at least an hour and a half. After calming him down somewhat, coffee was made available and we settled down to chat. He had heard from some of his friends on other ships that this 'new' dry dock was rather spectacular and efficient, but he wasn't convinced. He was of the old Teutonic school who firmly believed that the only people who could fix a German ship were his countrymen in Hamburg or Bremen, and this new company would take at least a week to repair his ship. I remained neutral and replied that I didn't know much about the work practices but had heard that they were very efficient and quick. I'm afraid that I then let the cat out of the bag when I informed him that, whilst the staff and in particular Len Laithwaite were cooperative, speedy and very, very good, the dock itself was very old. The actual bones of the dock were somewhat antiquated, they even opened the dry dock gates by hand, utilising capstans as in the old sailing ships when heavy ropes and anchor hawsers were heaved in using manpower. Those vertical rotating drums were powered by inserting capstan bars into the top edge of the drum and the men walking round and round the capstan in circles. Many a sea shanty was composed to be sung by the men who carried out this intensely hard physical work and are traditionally still sung at sea shanty festivals to this day. At this last comment, the Captain went berserk, damning the English for their unions, their inefficiency and their age-old practices, saying that he wished his owners had been more careful in picking this company to carry out his repair!

Eventually, after about an hour and a quarter, I asked for the anchor to be raised, and we proceeded the short distance from the anchorage to the entrance of the River Hull, where the dry dock was situated. In order to enter the dock, the ship had to be carefully placed very close to the Horsewash, an ancient slipway facility for literally washing and cooling the dray horses' hooves off after their work was completed delivering cargoes by wagon in the olden days. On dropping into the Horsewash, the view of the dry dock itself from the ship's wheelhouse is obscured by an office building ashore on the corner of the entrance to the River Hull, and the view was one of a fairly black hole, with nothing really in sight from the wheelhouse. This is where the trust between Captain and Pilot is stretched to the limit. This Captain had never been in the River Hull before, only passed it when en route to the upper reaches in the River Humber and was therefore unaware that there was anything round this 'blind' corner. His doubts came more to the fore when I asked him to get the crew on the foc's'le to put out a 'spring line' to the dolphin, a rope from the bows leading backwards to retard the ship's forward motion and help me to control the ship and swing her round to line up with the dock entrance. The crew on the bows could see the entrance of the dry dock from the foc's'le, but the Captain and I still could not!

They did comply partly due to encouragement from the dry dock crew on the dolphin and my request for this line to be put out, and we carried on swinging on this spring line attached to the dolphin to line up with and enter the dry dock. As I 'lifted' the stern of the ship round the corner, the dry dock came into view, and there on the walls either side of the entrance to the dock were the men operating the capstans with capstan bars, just as in the olden days in the times of sail and no mechanical power, walking round and round the capstans opening the dry dock gates BY HAND! By this time the Captain was in total disbelief with his head in his hands and crying, "No, no, no, surely you're not taking me in there Mr Pilot!"

The manoeuvre continued without problems, and after positioning her in the dry dock and settling her on the blocks, Len Laithwaite appeared and we exchanged greetings. The Captain had momentarily disappeared down below, and I informed Len of his misgivings. "Oh, I'll soon sort him out," was Len's typically brusque reply. "We'll have him out of here in 48 hours!" On returning to the wheelhouse and hearing this from Len, the Captain was still in disbelief and openly said to me when Len had gone to get on with his job that he simply didn't believe what he was being told. "No German shipyard could do this job in that time," he exclaimed, and after the Captain signed my pilotage note, I took my leave and left him in the care of Len and his workforce.

Now it didn't happen very often, but it did this time! Forty-eight hours later and a couple of other jobs in between, I got a call from the Duty Pilot issuing me with the job of taking that very same German ship out of Central Dry Dock to sea. When I boarded, the Captain greeted me with open arms, still saying that what had been done was not possible, and he apologised for not believing me at the outset. He was delighted and full of praise for the staff at the dry dock, vowing to tell all and sundry that if you wanted a good, efficient job done in double quick time, then the River Hull on the Humber was the place to go!

Sadly, the dry dock closed for good in the 1990s after Len's retirement, and after being a temporary home for the former Isle of Man steamer *Manxman* operating as a night club, it was eventually converted with a lot of ingenuity into the open-air auditorium that it is today.

Central Dry Dock.

Central Dry Dock Gates.

Saving Space?

Ship sizes are measured in what, to some, seem very confusing ways. One hears talk of massive 300,000-ton ships but what is the 'ton' referred to?

There are 'deadweight tons' which are usually applied when talking about large tankers and bulk cargo carriers, and there are 'gross tons', used when talking about large passenger ships or cruise liners. Without exception, all are used to the shipowner's advantage to make their ships appear as large and attractive as possible, mainly to impress and attract potential users, be they cargo shippers or passenger agents. A deadweight ton is obvious – it refers to the actual weight that any ship can actually carry before it sinks below its maximum load lines, and the gross ton is a measure of volume – 100 cubic feet is equal to one gross ton – and refers to physical size.

But there is one tonnage that escapes most landlubbers notice, and that is one of a 'space ton'. This magic figure is, or should I say *was*, used to calculate and decide how much cargo an old-fashioned dry cargo ship could contain below in her hatches. This space ton was 40 cubic feet and gave an indication of how much space there was down below in each of the multiple cargo spaces contained within a sophisticated cargo vessel of those days. It was also an indicator to the long-suffering Chief Officer, whose responsibility it was to fit all this cargo into the spaces down below, and what order to load it in.

Nowadays of course, everything seems to be carried in containers and pre-packed ashore before being loaded on to these massive lumps of ships that now carry most of the world's freight. But in the 'good old days' the space ton ruled when loading ships homeward bound for Europe. Outward bound to the Far East, the cargo was mainly heavy machinery and manufactured goods for the consumers in the less developed countries we sailed to, but homeward bound it was mainly raw materials from those countries and also an awful lot of plastic toys: cameras, luxury goods etc., and occasionally some heavy machinery from the more developed countries who were, at the time, starting to take over from the once mighty European heavy equipment manufacturers.

We used to distribute all this cargo with the heavy stuff low down in the ship to maintain stability, and the lighter stuff higher up where there was much more space. And of course, it all had to be accessible when we reached our discharging ports in Europe, no good having the last discharging port's cargo on top of the first port's cargo – difficult to get at it! None of the cargo ever arrived at the ship's side for loading in the order that made life easy, and we used to take some rather cheeky short cuts and employ all our wits to ensure that we loaded everything correctly.

One voyage loading the *Flintshire* in Yokohama, Japan on the homeward leg, we had been consigned to carry 17 Komatsu bulldozers to London, each weighing in at about 12 tons, and well-built with fairly heavy gauge steel shells and covers over the engines. These were assigned to one of the lower decks in the ship and duly loaded, positioned out towards the sides of the ship, and then well lashed down – these lumps were not the sort of thing one wanted to be moving about in the hatch when the ship hit the big swells in the Indian Ocean and the South Atlantic en route home.

Having previously been to Shanghai before proceeding to

Japan we had already loaded the whole of the refrigerated cargo spaces in No 4 Hatch of the ship in China and had plenty of stability, for that class of ship was well designed and very stable, so one could take some liberties with the stability, but not that many! Unfortunately, we didn't have any chilled or refrigerated cargo space left as we had completely filled it with frozen pork, eggs, prawns and other similar frozen cargo in Shanghai that needed below zero transportation temperatures. When the agent in Shimizu, Japan came to the ship and asked us if we could take some cultivated bonsai trees back to the United Kingdom from Kobe, we were at a bit of a loss. Consulting with the Chief Officer, I suggested that we ask our Chief Steward if there would be any space left in the ship's domestic fridge for the bonsai trees to be kept at the required shipping temperature – this was a very valuable cargo with a high freight rate and high revenue for the company, so we were somewhat loath to decline the shipment.

"How many are there?" asked the Chief Steward. "Forty-nine," replied the agent, and so it was agreed – 49 cases or cartons could fairly easily be swallowed in the large domestic fridge space of the ship.

Arriving in Kobe, we started to discharge the last of our outward-bound cargo. But as was usual, homeward-bound cargo to be loaded started arriving at the same time, and the customary state of confusion reigned. In the midst of all this confusion a very polite Japanese shipping agent arrived, announcing that the very valuable bonsai trees were at the foot of the gangway waiting to be loaded. I went to see the Chief Steward to warn him that we would like access to the domestic fridge, and would start bringing the cartons down to the catering area below decks for stowing. I went down to the quay and examined the shipment, the first pallet of which had been landed on the ship's deck and the stevedores had started to take them down through the accommodation to the ship's fridge area. There seemed to be an awful lot of these cartons on the lorry, and, with alarm bells ringing in my ears, I asked how many there were. "Ah, this first lorry, two more lorries to follow!"

Oops! The shipment was in fact 4.9 tons – about 200 cubic feet – not the 49 cases/cartons that we expected! Much egg on face, we had then to refuse the shipment as with a ship's crew of about 30, and 12 paying passengers to feed on the long trip home to the UK via the Cape of Good Hope, there just wasn't the space to accommodate all those beautiful little trees!

Some of the cargo we carried outward bound was slightly mystifying as well. There was a huge trade in battered and beaten-up old vehicles that we carried out to Singapore, all 'on deck' at 'shippers' risk'. It made the duty of the officer of the watch a little difficult as, after each watch at night, he had to go around the ship and check that all was well, and having to climb over these multiple vehicles and their lashings on the main and after decks of the ship was a little tortuous and sometimes at night, in heavy seas, dangerous! But it was good freight and all at no risk to the ship. We often wondered what happened to these MOT failures and positive wrecks of vehicles once they arrived, but this was explained to me by a passenger on the *Flintshire* one night after I had done my rounds on coming off watch at midnight. He was a Captain of one of the small inter-island traders of the Straits Steamship Company that traded around the South China Sea, based in Singapore. This Captain was still resident in the UK and was travelling back with us as a passenger after his leave to re-join his ship in Malaya. He was having a last cigarette before retiring, and we started to chat about the world in general. I commented on the state of some of these lorries, and he explained that they carried them onward to the great timber plantations of Borneo after they had been 'breathed on' by the engineering companies in Singapore. These wrecks were cannibalised, often three were made into two, they were lengthened, stiffened and given new life on the vast timber estates in Borneo. Whereas they couldn't be used on public roads in the UK, they were ideal for running around carrying huge loads of trees and sawn timber on the private estate roads in the Far East.

"You think these are wrecks?" he added. "You should see them when we carry them back from Borneo to be finally scrapped – the occasional one actually folds in half when we pick them up on our derricks to re-load them!"

Homeward bound, after Japan, we would go to Hong Kong to lay in the middle of the harbour on a mooring buoy to load yet more cargo – thousands of cartons of plastic goods – toys, flowers etc, and manufactured clothes, sweaters, shirts, pyjamas, T-shirts and more. These would arrive stacked so high on junks that it always amazed us that they survived the trip from wharf ashore to ship's side without toppling off into the harbour! However, it was all booked and had to be loaded.

On completing loading at any one port, the remaining space left in each compartment would be measured and calculated so that the Chief Officer would know where he had space to load cargo at the next loading port. For example, the space in the deck where I had loaded the bulldozers was not full – there was room in the space around and above the bulldozers, but that space was considered to be 'dead'.

On one morning in Hong Kong, I found the Chief Officer with his head in his hands at his desk, and when I asked him what the problem was, he simply said, "They've overbooked us again. Where the hell can I put all this stuff?" Junks were arriving at the rate of about five an hour and were already banked out on each side of the ship about four deep at every hatch. Space had to be left for loading in Singapore and Malaya, and we were getting really rather full. Proceeding onto the deck I went down and had a look around; cargo was being thrown into every available space as had been planned and things were getting very tight. I looked at the bulldozers nestling comfortably in the wings of No 5 Lower Tween Deck, all lashed down and taking up most of the space in that compartment. The engine compartment covers of the beasts were very substantial, so I thought – why not? Covering them in soft rattan mats which we carried in abundance to separate different cargoes, I instructed the stevedores to start loading behind and on top of the bulldozers, finishing off with a nice neat flat 'face' or wall of cartons visible from the middle of the hatch. All that was left visible to indicate that there were any bulldozers there were the inboard end of the multiple lashings that secured them for the voyage home. Dai Jones, our renowned and well-respected Chief Officer, happened to look down the hatch on his rounds later in the day, and asked where I had managed to put all the overbooked cartons. He was a little surprised to say the least when I explained, but at the same time unconcerned, as he took my word for it that the bulldozers were strong enough to bear the additional weight on top of them.

No more was said until we arrived in London some weeks later. We had arrived on our berth in the Royal Docks, and I was in the process of signing off the ship's articles to proceed home on leave. Christine, my wife, having driven up in our car to take me home for my well-deserved four weeks off. I was in the middle of handing over to my relief when Dai appeared at my cabin door with a huge grin on his face and asked me to come to the ship's office. There I was introduced to the buyer of the 17 Komatsu Bulldozers, who had come down to see his new purchase. Slightly embarrassed, I took the gentleman down to the appropriate space in No 5 Hatch, and we stood in the middle of the hatch. There was no sign of any bulldozers, so I nodded to the ends of the heavy wire lashings, still protruding from the wall of cartons. He looked a bit mystified, but I assured him that if he wanted to see his precious cargo, if he followed the wires, he would find them! They were discharged a couple of days later apparently, as expected totally undamaged and in perfect condition, much to everyone's relief!

MV *Flintshire.*
Gross reg tonnage:11,962 tons. Dead weight tonnage: 11,732 tons.

The Regulars

One of our pleasures when flying the hovercraft on the Cowes to Southampton route was meeting, greeting and getting to know the small army of regular passengers who joined us every morning and every evening. The design of the SR.N6 craft was such that Commander and passengers all travelled in the same compartment, and the intimacy generated was delightful, we felt close to them and it was reciprocated with cheerful banter always being exchanged when the weather was inclement. The 0725 in the morning from Cowes was always full, booked well in advance by an army of commuters who travelled daily to London and sometimes beyond to their place of work. Equally busy was the 0830, also from Cowes, carrying passengers to their places of work in Southampton and its immediate hinterland.

We got to know these people well and exchanged pleasantries with them every morning and evening. The mysteries of the life of the commuter were alien to most of us Hovercraft Commanders who had, for most of our working lives, lived either 'on the job' whilst at sea and after coming ashore, close to our place of work. I remember asking one of our regulars why he suffered what seemed to me to be the interminable travelling to and from his place of work in the City of London.

He explained quite simply that before he moved and relocated to the Isle of Wight from the outskirts of London, he would have to get up at around 0630 every morning, catch a packed commuter train at about 0800, and stand or be crammed into a compartment for an hour before walking to his office, where he arrived at 0915. The same tedious packed commute was repeated in reverse in the evening, and he arrived home stressed and tired out at about 7pm. His family life was blighted by the travelling, and although he lived on the leafy outskirts of the metropolis it was a real effort to take his family out at the weekends. His daughters were into horses and yearned for land and space to keep their own animals close at hand.

"Why move?" I asked.

His answer was simple and logical. Travelling from the island daily, he rose at 0615, left home at 0700, boarded the 0725 hovercraft to Southampton where, upon arrival, he was taken to Southampton Railway Station by the SeaSpeed bus. He then caught the 0805 non-stop service to Waterloo, arriving at 0920, walked to his office and was behind his desk at 0930. In the evening he left work at 1700, caught a train to Southampton and the 1900 service hovercraft back to Cowes, walking back into his own house at about 1945. He was able to sit on the train and catch up with work which he had previously had to do at home after returning from the hustle and bustle of the City each evening, and as he said, "The girls have their horses at home and I don't have to take the family out into the country every weekend – I *live* in the country!" The extra cost of the commute was more than covered by the difference between the extortionate council taxes in London and those of the island, and his quality of life was so much better that he felt a different person altogether.

Our regulars were extremely important to the success or otherwise of the service and the hostesses in the terminal were equally as keen to foster good relations with them and encourage them to stay with us. They started to introduce little benefits to these valued customers, simple things like coming to an arrangement with the local newsagents whereby they obtained daily newspapers for our regulars and would have them at the desk when they checked in for their early morning flight. One such regular was a retired Royal Navy Captain who had, after leaving the Navy, procured a job as an advisor and liaison officer between the Navy and Vosper Thorneycroft, one of the main Royal Navy ship builders, based at Woolston on the River Itchen. For Captain Philips, the commute to work every morning on the 0830 hovercraft and then a short hop across the Itchen on the floating bridge ferry to Vosper's yard at Woolston was quick and very convenient.

As one would expect of a man of his rank and upbringing, his daily morning reading delight was the *Daily Telegraph*, and invariably when we landed at Cowes on the 0800 return flight from Southampton, Captain Philips would be standing outside the terminal building looking his usual dapper self with his *Daily Telegraph* tucked under one arm, waiting to board the craft for the flight to Southampton. After the intensity of that first morning 'round trip', we would always try to snatch a cup of coffee at the terminal buffet after landing and before departing back for Southampton on the 0830 from Cowes, and Captain Philips would always politely ask if he may sit in the front seat alongside us. There he would sit and chat to us during the crossing (if we weren't too busy) and he would always comment, after reading the headlines of his *Telegraph*, about yet another car strike or the vagaries of the left-wing politicians and union bosses of the day.

The newspaper industry equally was not immune to strikes, and on one occasion the *Telegraph* itself was hit by a succession of strikes and did not appear. One of the hostesses in the terminal was a very vivacious and lovely young lady called Laura, who had a wonderful, impish sense of humour, and could respond to a situation when the opportunity presented itself. On the first morning of one of the *Telegraph* strikes, Laura collared me as I entered the terminal for my short coffee break between flights with a sparkle in her eyes and explained that she had procured a copy of the *Sun* for Captain Philips in place of his usual *Daily Telegraph*.

On returning to the craft to wind up the engine prior to taking off, I encountered Captain Philips on the apron where he asked me if he could take his preferred seat at the front of the craft alongside me, and he mentioned with apparent bemusement that he had been furnished with the *Sun* rather than his usual *Daily Telegraph*. Sticking to his usual routine he waited until we had lifted off, taking special delight in watching us handle the craft while negotiating the tricky hovercraft channel out of, and clear of, Cowes Harbour, and then the daily routine procedure would begin before opening his newspaper. From his waistcoat pocket would appear his monocle which would then be screwed firmly into his right eye. The main headline of the paper would be commented on and then a foray into the inner pages would follow. That particular morning there was a particularly cheesy and typical *Sun*-style headline which was brushed over with some disdain, and then the paper was opened up to reveal Page 3. At the sight of the *Sun's* Page 3 trademark photograph of a semi-naked young lady, the eyebrows shot up, the monocle dropped out, and an audible sharp intake of breath was heard. "Oh Good Heavens Jeremy – have you seen this?!" There was, however, a wry smile on the face of Captain Philips, and the amusing postscript to this little tale is that for ever after that, his morning newspaper order was changed to the *Telegraph* AND the *Sun*.

Standard 38-seat SR.N6 departing Cowes Hoverport,

'Stretched' SR.N6 Mk 1 (S) – Lengthened by 10-foot section placed in the middle of the craft, to accommodate 56 passengers.

The 'Friendly Bears'

The use of VHF radio to talk to other ships and shore stations was a major advance in communications in the 1960s, and the ability to make and receive telephone calls when in range of shore stations dotted around the coastlines of most major countries was a revolution. Unfortunately, this radio communication system became used for many of the wrong reasons, and the phrase 'VHF-assisted collision' became all too familiar. With the introduction of foreign crews into major shipping concerns, their training and practices became all too familiar and created some concern among the professionals who had to deal with them at first hand. Of course, any problem such as this had its funny side, and there were many stories of exchanges between ships that came to light.

Equally amusing were some of the comments blurted out in – not so much panic – but a state of shock after something untoward had happened. One day, there were some ten ships all inward bound for 'up-river' destinations in pretty thick fog and all assembling in the South Channel off Hull, and we were awaiting handing over our charges to our up-river colleagues. This procedure could be fraught with danger with the up-river Pilots deciding amongst themselves who was to take which ship, and we Lower Station Pilots trying to keep control of our ships while being 'sluiced' up the river by the very strong following tidal current.

In amongst all this apparent mayhem would be the sewage carriers without Pilots, who had their own Pilotage Exemption Certificates allowing them to pilot their own ships. These ships plied their trade from Goole Docks, where they loaded raw untreated sewage from the vast housing estates in Leeds, carried to Goole by canal barge and loaded on to these sewage ships. These vessels incidentally were romantically named after some of the reservoirs in the beautiful parts of the Pennines and Derbyshire peaks: *Scammonden*, *Thruscross* and *Anglezarke* to name just three, and these ships were affectionately known to all and sundry as 'The Bovril Boats'. However, on this particular day, one of these Bovril Boats in the line of other ships proceeding up-river failed to realise that the ship ahead of him had slowed down prior to changing Pilots, and promptly ran into his stern. This elicited a prompt report from the Pilot of the damaged ship, which simply came over the air as, "Hey Hull Radio, the shit boat's just twatted me up the arse!"

Often, when on the long haul down-river in the wee small hours, Pilots and Masters of ships would while away the hours in conversation about anything and everything, generally putting the world to rights. As always, the VHF would be on listening watch, and one night while I was piloting the *Union Diamond* out to sea, a call was heard – this ambiguous transmission contained only the words, "Ship on my starboard bow, what are you doing?" This elicited a smile and a laugh from the Master and myself, and we started to swap VHF stories. I related the 'Bovril Boat' incident, and he replied with a couple of stories that tickled my sense of humour.

The Master told of one night listening to transmissions from a container ship inward-bound for Felixstowe becoming increasingly more agitated as he got closer to the approaches. The Cork Anchorage is situated to the north of the entrance channel to the port, and for some reason the Master of the container ship got it into his head that another ship was leaving the anchorage and crossing his path.

According to the International Rules for the Prevention of Collision at Sea, although the inward-bound container ship was the 'give way vessel', the ship which he surmised was apparently crossing ahead of him should give way as the water was too shallow for the inward-bound container ship to yield, as he could run aground if he did indeed 'give way'. After several calls to the mystery ship in the anchorage and the increasing agitation in the voice of the inward-bound container ship's Master, someone else who had been listening pointed out to him that the ship in question was in fact anchored, and from then on there was a stunned silence.

But the Master's second story took the cake. In the long boring hours of keeping a watch at sea, it was often an innocent diversion to ask over the VHF radio if there was anyone out there who "fancied a chat?" This initial call was made on Channel 16, the international calling and safety channel, and on receiving replies, then suggesting that the conversation would be held on another ship-to-ship channel. On this particular night, whilst travelling across the north coast of Norfolk bound to Rotterdam from Kings Lynn in the Wash, in near perfect North Sea conditions – flat calm, no wind and excellent visibility – the VHF on the ship suddenly sprang into life with a polite request from another lonely watchkeeping officer: "Are there any 'Friendly Bears' out there?"

The Master told me that he reached forward to pick up the handset of his VHF radio set to reply and start a chat, but before he could reply, a very hoity toity pompous voice blasted on the air waves informing the first ship that, "Don't you know you are contravening Section 4 of the Radio Telegraphy Act 1957, Subsection 8, paragraph 12 [or similar words to that effect]." and the voice went on and on to list various charges that could be brought against the perpetrator of this evil deed on the radio airwaves.

Now it has to be noted that, at that time, there were many radio stations around the coasts of all the countries of the world, providing radio telephone links to the shore, and they offered a valuable service to the marine fraternity. These stations were operated by the Post Office in the UK and were highly respected instruments of life at sea. 'Link calls' connected to the shore telephone systems could be made via these stations when a ship was in VHF radio range of them, not only to company offices but also to loved ones at home, and they made life at sea much more palatable. However, they were sometimes manned by rather officious operators, and in this case, this is where this outburst had probably come from – correctly and according to the regulations – but what the heck, it was a quiet night, no radio traffic at all and a perfect opportunity for a 'round robin chat' amongst lonely ships' Watch Officers.

The Master said that he just froze after this transmission and wondered what on earth the response would be to this rather testy outburst. If the original transmitter of the request had been terribly rude and told the operator at the coast station to go away in a vulgar fashion, it would not have been funny. But all the original first voice said in a questioning manner was, "You're not a 'Friendly Bear' are you?"

Within minutes there was the biggest round robin in progress on the VHF, several ships having heard the outburst and wanting to join in for a chat, accompanied by comments such as, "Who was that miserable bleeder?" and other such rather disparaging comments. It was decided that it would have been the Duty Operator at Humber Radio with nothing better to do than tear a strip off a perfectly innocent ship's officer for a very minor offence, but the conversation soon turned to much more pleasant content, and whiled away the wee small, lonely hours of a dark night on the North Sea.

As a postscript, most of these coast radio stations now no longer exist, overtaken and made redundant by satellite and mobile phone technology, but at the time they were a very welcome addition to 'Life at Sea'.

The Vagaries of Immigration Control

Particularly during the very last part of my working career, I experienced many differing levels of immigration control when travelling around the world. Most of us have had to suffer silly questions being asked when applying for entry visas into various countries and have run the gauntlet of some pretty aggressive questioning at the border control desks of other countries as well.

It was normal procedure when a ship arrived at a foreign port for the Purser, Radio Officer or Chief Steward (whoever was officiating as ship's Purser at the time) to meet with the country's immigration officials, bearing all identity documents of officers and crew on board the ship, and for clearance to be obtained for all the ship's company in a short but nevertheless formal manner in very quick time. *Free pratique* would then be granted and then all the crew were able to go ashore to savour the delights of the country they were visiting.

Arrival in The People's Republic of China in the 1960s was, however, somewhat different and quite an experience. The schedule for the 'L'-service ships in Glen Line, of which the *Flintshire* was one and on which I served later in my time with Blue Funnel and Glen Line, took us from London direct to Singapore, on to Hong Kong, Manila and then to Shanghai. The entry of the ship and its crew into Communist China in those days was a fairly fraught procedure, with an arrival inspection carried out with heavily armed guards in attendance. All the officers and crew were herded into their respective saloons and mess rooms while these armed guards, accompanied by allocated ship's officers, searched absolutely everything that was in cabins, public rooms, galleys, storerooms and even the cargo hatches and the engine room. Personal effects in cabins were rifled through in the search for any material that was considered to be of a subversive nature, and in order to protect our own personal privacy we used to land all personal papers, letters from family etc. in Hong Kong for storage at the offices of the ship's agents before we went to China.

On one occasion I had been loaned a copy of George Orwell's *Animal Farm*, that famous parody on Communism, and had actually forgotten to land it with all my other personal effects. It was not until after we had departed China that I realised that it had been there during the search and can only assume that if indeed it had been spotted, the guard in question had not understood its significance, otherwise I could quite easily have languished for some time in a Chinese prison.

During the 'enlightened period' of the late-1960s, Blue Funnel and Glen Line supplied their ships with a film projector and four feature films to entertain us on the long sea passages. On arrival in Singapore, we would land these four films and were then given two films to entertain us around the coast of the Far Eastern countries we visited while 'port hopping'. On one memorable occasion our two films allocated for the coasting period by some extremely bright spark were Walt Disney's *Jungle Book* and *The Yangtse Incident*. Needless to say, the latter of these films had to be landed in Hong Kong so as not to cause an international incident, and we spent a couple of nights anchored off Shanghai waiting to enter the port watching *Jungle Book*, while under the inscrutable oriental gaze of stony-faced Chinese guards peering through the saloon windows at these filthy bourgeoisie capitalists falling about laughing at a cartoon film.

The other problem with arriving in China from Manila was that the Philippines in those days was considered to be a highly possible source of cholera, and before we were allowed to proceed to our berth, everyone had to provide a stool sample which was then checked and cleared by a Chinese port health doctor who stayed on board until this process was complete. Slightly distasteful probably, but one could understand that with the enormous hordes of people in China, and particularly Shanghai, a cholera outbreak would have been disastrous in those days of the Communist era.

Entry in to the United States of America was equally complicated in those days: McCarthyism was still prominent in the minds of all Americans, and the witch hunts of the '50s were still all too fresh in the memory. As a midshipman I had served on the *Telamon*, one of the ships on the Barber Blue Sea run jointly operated by Blue Funnel. These ships never came to the UK, and circumnavigated the globe in an easterly direction trading from the eastern seaboard of the United States and the Gulf of Mexico, across the Atlantic calling at Alexandria and Jeddah in the Middle East before proceeding across the Indian Ocean to Malaya, Indonesia and then to Hong Kong. Discharge of all cargoes would be completed here; the ship would then dry dock before proceeding to the Philippines to load sugar, back to Hong Kong and on to Japan to load consumables before crossing the Pacific, transiting the Panama Canal and calling at Kingston, Jamaica before arriving back on the eastern seaboard of the USA at New York.

Our arrival in our first US port of call, New York, was subject to what could only be called a Spanish-style inquisition by the gentlemen from the Immigration

Department of the FBI. Again, we would all be paraded in front of an interview panel that consisted of two or three gentlemen who were archetypal 'all-American boys'. The uniform was apparent – loud check jackets, trousers of pastel shades that were particularly popular with the golfing fraternity, shirts with collar pins clipping their shirt collars together behind their ties and brash tie pins that could only have originated in the States. Coupled with the crew-cut hairstyle of the day, these were true all-American boys. We never detected the tell-tale bulge under the jacket, but none of us would have been surprised to discover a Colt 45 hand gun secreted somewhere about their personage.

Teucer, sister ship to the *Telamon*.

The interview panel would be seated across the end of the officers' saloon, and the Captain of the ship would sit with them, introducing each officer in turn. Our Captain on the *Telamon* was outwardly suave and sophisticated, but deep down there lurked a very nervous character. The cigarette holder with a lighted Pall Mall and the apparent devil may care attitude hid an underlying uncertainty in almost everything he undertook. The possibility that someone may say something that riled the immigration officials and upset the whole procedure was of concern to him as Master – anything that delayed or disrupted the smooth transition of the ship was a concern.

Each of us was questioned in turn with a series of seemingly pointless questions, some of which were so silly they beggared belief. The two that stick in my mind were grouped together towards the end of the charade and ran thus:

"Are you now, or have you ever been a member of the Communist Party?" and;

"Is there any insanity in your family?"

The first of the two questions was rather pointless – if anybody had ever joined that party, would they admit it to an American immigration official? A lot of people found the second question very amusing, but in order to obtain the desired shore pass, which was the object of the whole exercise, a bland answer was provided in the negative.

The instance that springs to mind happened during one entry process into the States and involved a Geordie 4th Engineer who had flown out to join the ship in the Middle East, and therefore had not been to the States before. He was blessed with that wonderful dry Geordie sense of humour, an impish mind and intolerance of the ridiculous – to say he didn't suffer fools gladly would have been an understatement. He obviously found this whole pantomime unbearably silly, and I could see in his face what was on his mind as we queued patiently before the inquisition panel.

When his turn came to face the music, he answered all the questions with the usual bland replies, until asked, "Is there any insanity in your family?"

The answer came as a very clear, "Yes!" All the FBI boys' heads shot up and stared at the engineer, who stood impassively in front of them, and I thought our suave and sophisticated Captain was going to have a heart attack or apoplexy at least. Quizzed as to what this insanity was, the engineer simply replied, "My sister married a bloody Yank!"

It was a noticeable fact that it was only he, of all the ship's officers and crew, that did *not* get issued with a shore pass!

Coming Ashore!

In the early-1970s, the cruising cutters that had served the Humber Pilot service for many, many years were coming to the end of their useful lives. The raison d'être of the service was to provide a Pilot at any time, day or night, 365 days a year to any ship that required a Pilot. These fine cutters were stationed off the East Yorkshire coast at the entrance to the river and held a reserve of Pilots aboard for boarding on to ships as they approached. In reverse of course they were there to also 'land' Pilots from outward-bound ships, and to accommodate them until such time as they were either taken off or re-boarded again on inward ships for the docks and berths on the river.

They were also there of course to provide a training ground for the Pilots of the future, the cutters themselves being crewed by Pilot apprentices undergoing their initial training in the little 'punts' that transferred the Pilots from cutters to ships and serving their apprenticeship, accompanying Pilots on the river to learn their trade.

However, the cutters were beginning to show their age, and the last of the old ladies, the *William Fenton*, had a boiler defect that proved terminal. The cost of replacing her boiler or replacing the main engine with a diesel unit was to prove far too expensive, and an alternative had to be found. Many of the pilot services around the world were operated from shore bases, and the decision on the Humber was to follow suit and come ashore at Spurn Point, that elusive and constantly moving spit of land that partially protected the entrance to the Humber Estuary. It was the obvious choice for a shore base, close to the gateway of access to the many ports and jetties on the estuary and accessible by road from the Pilot Office in Hull. I don't think anyone in the service was under any illusion that the transition from sea to shore was going to be easy, but the newly appointed Pilotage Operations Manager – a very senior Pilot who had many years' service under his belt and an intimate knowledge of the workings of the job – was more than up for the challenge, and he set about having plans drawn up for the creation of an up-to-date shore base. This also entailed the conversion of the former officers' mess on Spurn into accommodation for the Pilots.

Spurn Point had been an important part of the coastal sea defences during both the world wars, and there existed many large and substantial gun mountings dotted around the point end which would provide adequate foundations for any structures that needed building. The new Pilotage Operations Manager set about dragging the service into the 20th century, away from practices of the previous 450 years of the existence of the Humber Pilot Service. His plans were ambitious and needed a lot of negotiation with the Port Authority to extract the funds needed for such progress, but he persevered and we ended up with one of the finest shore stations in the country.

The building of the control tower itself was a major undertaking. The Pilots would occupy the third floor, with the coastguards above us on the fourth floor, the latter surprisingly without any radar coverage at all or even the ability to 'crib' our radars to observe any goings on to seaward. First and second floors would be taken up with computer servers and electronics, and a service kitchen for the Pilots on duty in the tower. All this would be topped on the fifth floor by a small observatory for the 'twitchers', the bird watchers who visited the point in their droves to pursue their hobby.

Construction was commenced and some time after the first and second floors were actually up, a gentleman from the local council offices arrived saying that he hadn't been advised of the completion of the foundations for this quite large structure. It was in fact being built on an absolutely massive 8-inch gun mounting, and the site foreman looked at this rather worried looking little council official who was demanding to see the extent of the foundations. The foreman simply handed the official a shovel, saying that they had dug down some 15 feet alongside this huge concrete base slab with a JCB digger, and couldn't find the bottom of it. He merely then asked the official to let them know if he found the bottom of the concrete block!

The control tower at Spurn.

While all this construction was going on, visual and radar coverage of the approaches to the river previously observed from the bridge of the cutter itself while outside on station had to be maintained. Now that the cutter was moored inside Spurn Point, a temporary arrangement had to be found so that the approaches could be monitored, and ships guided to where the launches were working and boarding ships. More innovations were required, and up came the idea of a Portacabin mounted on top of one of the former gun battery ammunition store rooms, and the radars from the cutter were then placed in this 'hut' with the radar antennae stuck on to tall masts alongside this new 'control centre' so that they could 'see' over the top of the sand dunes. This system stood for many months while the tower was being built and worked well.

The blue Portacabin 'hut' perched atop a former ammunition store; temporary arrangement for controlling the approaches.

A 'Spurn Committee' was formed to man this new arrangement, and consisted of six of the very senior Pilots who had also taken part in the organisation of the whole new system and worked with the Operations Manager to set up something that was, for the Humber, entirely new. These senior Pilots took on the role of 'Pilot Masters' and ran the service minute by minute from this small enclave on the windswept end of the Spurn Peninsula. Issuing of jobs from the docks in Hull continued to be arranged by the staff at the Pilot Office in Hull, and the jobs from the docks on the South Bank – Immingham and Grimsby – continued to be looked after by the staff at the Grimsby Pilot Office on the Royal Dock.

One of these Pilot Masters was a lovely chap, John Ward, a man with whom one wouldn't want to argue with but who was in fact a big soft teddy bear of a man, a veritable gentle giant. John had a voice that could shake mountains, enormous in volume and with a broad local accent. In order for the system to work, the Pilot Master needed some assistance, and the job of a 4-hour 'lookout' fell more often than not to the more junior Pilots who were on the turn list, as it was a job they could do when there were too many large ships to cater for that they couldn't do because of the draft and size restriction placed on those younger men.

Spending four hours cooped up in that tiny Portacabin with John Ward was, to say the least, a bit of an onerous task, and it fell to me quite a number of times during my early months on the job. John's booming voice reverberated around the walls of that small enclave of the 'cabin on stilts' and the walls would pulsate owing to the volume of his voice, causing all around him to end up somewhat deafened by the end of their watch! There were the unkinder in the service who said that John didn't even need a radio to contact the distant incoming ships, all he had to do was go outside and yell at them!

A long jetty for the launches was to be built inside the lee of the point to allow the new 20-knot launches to berth safely before taking on Pilots and transporting them out to the ships to be boarded, and also of course to land them ashore after they had been taken off the ships outward bound.

Building the jetty at Spurn.

This whole construction took quite a time, and I started in the service in 1975, midway through this process. The defunct and boiler-less cutter was moored to buoys inside the point, and we used to travel back and forth to the cutter being used as temporary brief accommodation for Pilots while they waited to be boarded or to go home. 'Punts', as they were known, from the cutter would come to the shore and take Pilots from the disused Admiralty Jetty when there was sufficient water for these small boats to get to it. The range of the tide was such that this was only possible for around four hours each tide, so an alternative had to be found. Totally undaunted, the Operations Manager commandeered a length of disused floating pipeline from the operators of the tanker buoy at Spurn and moored it to the shore in an arc pointing out across the water. We then made our way along this 'cakewalk' to the waiting punt to be transported out to the cutter moored some 400 metres away.

Temporary access arrangement to the cutter at low water. The floating pipe with a 'punt' at the end taking Pilots on board. The edge of the Admiralty Jetty can be seen at the extreme left of the picture.

We had many a 'fun walk' along that pipe when the weather turned a bit nasty, sometimes getting soaked and arriving on the cutter to be boarded with wet feet and feeling a little woozy! That pipe could certainly 'perform' when there was a chop on the river. But early one morning the whole of the service was brought to a peremptory halt when our local grey seal, very originally nicknamed 'Sammy', decided to use the pipe for a snooze and a rest. Seals can be vicious animals, and to try to disturb a seal can be fraught with the danger of being quite badly bitten. Sammy, however, refused to be goaded off the pipe, and for a time all operations came to a halt. Then one of the apprentices who was operating the punt came up with a brainwave. Why not try to entice Sammy off the pipe with some of Salmonella Stan's revolting bacon sandwiches – not the best of fare for the Pilots, and 'built' by our rather unsanitary steward aboard the cutter. But surely

Sammy would like to try them?

They returned to the cutter and came back with a stack of the unappetising and uneaten sandwiches from a couple of hours before, and by tossing them into the river away from the end of the pipeline, finally managed to tempt Sammy off the pipe so that normal service could be resumed!

The tower, jetty and all associated works were finally completed at the beginning of 1976, and we moved in to assume our place ashore and to work the station with increasing efficiency for the ships we served. There were many times that Sammy returned to plague us, but he never managed to quite disrupt the boardings and landings of Pilots as much as he did on that morning when he stopped the service just about completely!

Spurn Point with control tower to the right of the lighthouse, and the jetty on the extreme left of the photograph.

Cuddle from a Grateful Passenger!

As part of the contribution of the hovercraft industry into 'island life' on the Isle of Wight, we in SeaSpeed and those of our colleagues of Hovertravel provided an extra arm to the emergency services of the island. SeaSpeed ran a daily service of scheduled passenger services to Southampton from Cowes, and Hovertravel ran from Ryde to Southsea, throughout the year, but our second craft that was on standby in case of breakdowns of the service craft was also available for any sudden event that needed dealing with urgently. Some of these cases provided us with huge satisfaction that, when called upon, we could respond with high-speed help.

The Commander's daily duty roster included one man on standby around the clock. This man would also provide radar cover for the service craft in the event of night flights or foggy conditions, when two men were needed to operate the craft safely. Often days would go by without the services of the extra man on standby being needed, but occasionally we contributed to island life, and indeed the saving of life on the Solent in some memorable ways.

I was on standby one day in the spring when the phone went at my home; I was needed for a quick dash to the mainland and it didn't matter what I was dressed in. "Just get yourself down here asap!" I was cutting the grass at home, and I hopped onto my moped, dressed resplendent in mucky old gardening gear and was at the terminal in five minutes to find the engine of the craft already running – the Duty Engineer having thoughtfully started it for me in readiness for a quick getaway. An ambulance arrived under 'blue lights' on the pad from St. Mary's Hospital in Newport at the same time as I did, and a doctor and two nurses, together with a very seriously ill premature baby in an incubator were quickly boarded on the craft. Without delay we were off at maximum speed, and on arrival in Southampton some 16 minutes later we were met by another ambulance which quickly took the baby and medical staff to the Southampton General Hospital.

I returned to Cowes taking a few 'early comers' for the next scheduled service flight with me and went home again to continue mowing the lawn. About an hour and a half later I was summoned again, this time in not quite so much of a hurry, and I had the task of transporting the new baby's 'mummy' on a stretcher across the water to join her premature baby. Her blood was required so that the medical staff could give it to the baby to hopefully ensure its survival. Such little trips provided us with much satisfaction and made us feel that we really were providing a vital service to the islanders who had to suffer us waking them up every morning when we left Cowes in a cloud of spray and not inconsiderable noise!

We also on occasion were asked by the coastguard to join very basic search and rescue operations, if they did not interfere too much with our daily passenger carrying routines. Between the mainland and the island was the notorious Brambles Bank – a trap for unsuspecting yachtsmen unfamiliar with the area. Quite often we would come across a yacht high and dry on the bank and, although the coastguards could see the yacht from their watch tower on Calshot Spit, they couldn't get to them or contact them to see if there was any immediate danger to life. On those occasions they would ask us to stop by and check if the yacht and its occupants were alright. This was pre-mobile phone days and VHF radio sets were not commonly fitted to yachts. We of course being totally amphibious, could approach to within a matter of a few feet away from the unfortunate yacht and make sure everything was OK until they re-floated on the next rising tide.

On occasions we would run out an anchor for them, and sometimes we were asked the impossible, "Can you tow me off?"; "Can you take me ashore, I've got a train to catch?" but generally we could just relay messages to the coastguards and advise as to whether there was any imminent danger to the occupants of the yacht.

Other duties that we provided were sometimes a little bizarre. The island provided a site for one of 'Her Majesty's Hotels for Naughty Boys' – the large prison at Parkhurst. We got to know quite a few of the Prison Officers there as the SeaSpeed staff teamed up with Vosper Thorneycroft's drawing/design office staff based on the island to form a cricket team, which played in the island's limited over match league. Many a happy time was enjoyed in the warder's social club at Parkhurst after a cricket match at their ground in Newport. We did, however, sometimes meet up with some of these fine chaps in an official capacity in the dead of night.

HMP Parkhurst was the home for naughty boys, but HMP Albany on the same site as Parkhurst was a top security facility, and many a really naughty boy was housed at Her Majesty's pleasure in there. Occasionally, it was deemed necessary to transfer these top security prisoners to other facilities on the mainland, and we would be called out very surreptitiously in the wee small hours to provide transport for this procedure. Two of us would be rung up, one to fly the craft and one to operate the radar, and we would be briefed in the terminal before take-off. We never knew our destination before we commenced the flight and would be told only after we had departed the pad where we were to land and transfer the 'passenger'. Neither did we ever know, at the time, who we were transporting, as once the engine was running, we were required to avert our gaze while the passenger was brought on board, and then we took off to our destination. This could be anywhere, and the authorities rang the changes so that strict security could be maintained. Apart from our usual landing pad in Southampton, we occasionally ended up on Hovertravel's pad at Southsea, the slipway at HMS *Daedulus* where the Interservices Hovercraft Unit was based, and on one occasion on the car ferry slipway in Portsmouth Harbour itself. We sometimes found out who our mystery passenger had been a few days after the event, but sometimes we never knew and it would remain a mystery.

On one occasion when I was on standby, I was rung up at 2230 one evening, and to the surprise of the senior Commander, I was not there at the end of my phone. He was mystified as I had always tried to be as diligent and responsible as I possibly could be, and he said to his wife that it was not like me to be missing when I was wanted. As his house was literally just around the corner from where we lived, he, at his wife's suggestion, walked round to see that my car was not on the drive, and the penny dropped that I had presumably taken my heavily pregnant wife to the hospital at Newport. This was indeed the case as she had gone into labour at about 2200 that evening.

My first inkling that something was amiss was when I was subsequently rung at 0330 in the morning by the hospital to announce the arrival of our first born – a son weighing in at a healthy eight pounds. I asked if I could come straight away to see both wife and son and was asked just to give them a few minutes to let them clean them both up. On approaching the hospital at Newport, which was directly across the main Cowes to Newport road from HMP Parkhurst, I was stopped at a police road block and asked where I thought I was going at that time of the morning. I explained, and after a search of my car and removal of some rope from the back of the car, I was provided with a police motorcycle escort to the gates of the hospital.

On emerging some two hours later from St Mary's, having held my new-born son and settled my wife down to sleep after her ordeal, I left the hospital grounds to return home to Cowes. On reaching the road block I faced a barrage of questions: "How's the wife? How much did the little lad weigh? What are you going to call him then?" etc. When I enquired as to the purpose of all the extra security, I was told of the prison riots which had been going on all that night of the 26/27th August 1972, to which I had been completely oblivious.

The next morning, the senior Commander contacted me and firstly enquired after my wife and new baby as he and his wife had guessed when I hadn't been at home that what indeed had happened, had happened. He then told me about my absence, which had initially caused some surprise and concern, and asked if I could come in and help out that morning as the other four Commanders had been out during the night ferrying extra prison officers and police across from the mainland to bolster the staff at Parkhurst.

It was some five months after the cross-Solent dash with premature baby and later the mother as well, that I landed at Cowes one Sunday morning after a routine service run to Southampton, and was told by the Beach Master that I had two visitors. It was the same baby and her mother that I had transported some five months earlier on that worrying day, and they had simply come to say thank you. The little girl, named Jemimah, was now a beautiful healthy five-month-old, and had survived a very traumatic delivery and first few weeks of life. Back in those days the survival rate for premature babies was nowhere as near successful as that of today, and I like to think that the service we provided that day was just a small contribution to that little girl's chances. I will never forget being able to hold Jemimah and give her a little cuddle, nor the lovely hug and kiss I got from her mum!

BHC SR.N6 Mk 1 (S) *009*, GH 2014,
The *Sea Hawk*, taking off from the pad at Cowes.

These Boots are Made for Marching

It's funny how your mind wanders at the strangest times, and how a little thing can jog the grey cells to bring memories flooding back. I had just settled the ship in the lock at King George Dock after bringing her from her berth, and we were waiting to be dropped down to 'river level' before proceeding out to sea. The vessel was a regular runner to Hull, the old man a real toff, quite confident and unruffled by the actions of his Pilot, and quite happy for us to 'get on with it' without interfering in our job. Mind you, the ship was a dream to handle with her bridge wing controls for the rudder, 700 horse power bow thruster, and her pitch propellor, even if she swings the opposite way to most conventional ships when one puts the engines astern, which is termed as being 'left-handed'. With a perfect view along the ship's side, and all controls at your fingertips on a splendidly designed console, it was a delight of a job to do. It suddenly, however, dawned on me that the ship I had just put in the lock, 140 metres long, 19.2 metres beam, and drawing some 8.2 metres, was slightly bigger than the standard Blue Funnel 'A'-class ships of the late-1940s and early-'50s. Alfred Holt and Company's Blue Funnel and Glen Line fleet had been decimated during the Second World War, and these fine 'A'-class ships had been the backbone of the post-war rebuilding and regeneration programme, and I had served on them as a Midshipman, and subsequently as a Deck Officer, in the 1960s.

The thing that really brought me up with a round turn was the size of the crew. On the bridge for the whole manoeuvre from berth to lock had been myself as the Pilot, and the Captain. Forward was the First Mate with two deckhands, and aft was the Bosun with another sailor. The whole thing had been achieved without tugs, and with less bodies in total than there used to be on the foc's'le of an 'A'-class ship in 1961. I remember those days with great affection – Chief Officer and a Middie, Bosun and Chippy, at least two ABs, a Senior Ordinary Seaman, a Junior Ordinary Seaman, and probably a Deck Boy as well for good measure – those were the days! And that was only the foc's'le gang; there was a main deck gang of three men as well to handle the heavy wire spring lines. That was for the traditional Blue Funnel tie-up – seven parts of rope and five parts of wire each end of the ship. I would like to see the reaction from a modern-day Berthing Master if you told him that that was what you were sending to the shore when tying up in this day and age!

Still, things have progressed, and the modern-day ship with its automation and tension winches for mooring ropes can cope just as well, but somehow it just ain't the same. The cheerful banter from the all-Liverpool crew has gone, replaced by the strange sounds of Filipinos trying to talk to their Indian and Chinese crew mates in a form of Pidgin English that is difficult for even an Englishman to understand.

But I digress, what really came to mind while sitting in the lock was an occasion when I was coasting the *Autolycus* from Liverpool to Glasgow, Swansea, and back to Birkenhead. As part of a cultural exchange with our friends in Her Majesty's 'Grey Funnel Line', we had accompanying us as an observer, a Sub-Lieutenant from a destroyer, who had come to see how the 'other half' managed. He really was a super chap from excellent stock, beautifully spoken – no 'jolly Jack Tar' this one!

Arriving in Glasgow, we were approaching the dock, and the tugs appeared in their usual cloud of steam and smoke.

Time for 'stand by' – crew to be summoned to stations for making tugs fast and berthing. As the Bridge Midshipman I was instructed to 'blow for stations' (three blasts on a pea whistle) and after the briefest of delays, the crew were forward and aft. Our Sub-Lieutenant was obviously looking rather concerned, and I asked if there was something troubling him. He enquired when the crew were going to stations, and I replied that they were already there. Now this was 1964, and the crews had been reduced somewhat, but there were the usual half a dozen or so on the foc's'le, and I was somewhat bemused as to our naval friend's problem. He asked where the rest of the crew were, to which I replied, "Aft," and yet he still couldn't believe that we could manage with just this handful of bodies.

I suppose one could not blame him – on my first trip to sea on the *Aeneas* in 1961 I had witnessed the spectacle of a 'Daring'-class destroyer berthing next to us in Port Said to await the next southbound convoy through the Suez Canal. We had been amazed to see what appeared to be hundreds of crew members running up and down the decks of the warship, literally 'handing' the mooring ropes – no winches there, just sheer manpower. For our subby to see this merchant ship, with, to him, so few crew, about to complete a fairly tight manoeuvre into the dock at Glasgow must have filled him with foreboding.

He never ceased to keep us amused with his stories of his life working for 'The Queen', and his naivety about life outside the Royal Navy was quite illuminating, keeping us entertained for hours. We did eventually manage to get him partly educated into the ways of 'real life at sea', but not before a few hiccups.

The first, and most amusing little incident with our

'subby', was on his first night watch at sea. The First Officer had palmed him off onto the Second and Third Officers' watch, probably to keep him out of his hair, and we had just nicely cleared Liverpool Bar outward bound for the Clyde at about 2300. The Chief Officer, 4th Officer and myself were keeping the 8-12, and at one bell, quarter to midnight, I flitted off to call out the lads for the 12-4. The 2nd Officer and 3rd Officer were half conscious when I entered their rooms, and apart from telling me to go away in a disgusting fashion, were quite civil! As a Middie you came to expect these endearments when calling people for double watches after only a couple of hours in their bunks. Our Sub-Lieutenant was a totally different kettle of fish. Thanking me profusely he leapt from his bunk and commenced to dress. Returning to the bridge to complete the ritual concocting of tea for the oncoming watch, and, dispensing same to the bleary-eyed 2nd and 3rd Officers on their arrival in the wheelhouse, I observed that there was a noticeable absence of the 'Royal Navy'.

The 2nd and 3rd Officers had of course donned usual night time watch-keeping gear of slacks and sweater, and were already on the bridge taking over the watch in the wheelhouse. The First Officer was handing over the conning of the ship to the 2nd Officer, and the 4th Officer was handing over the navigational side of things to the 3rd Officer. At precisely 30 seconds to midnight, the Sub-Lieutenant appeared in the wheelhouse resplendent in full naval battle dress, collar and tie, Royal Navy cap planted squarely on his head, and wearing the biggest pair of boots the Navy could build. These boots weren't from the Army and Navy Stores, these were built at Cammell Lairds and launched. He marched across the wheelhouse, directly underneath which was situated the Captain's sleeping cabin, approached the 2nd

Officer, sprang to attention, saluted and asked what he should do.

As the whistle from the old man's voice pipe popped off its end in the wheelhouse and bounced around on the deck in response to the furious 'blowing' from the other end beside the Captain's bed, all five of us said simultaneously (but too late of course), "Go and take those ruddy boots off before you wake the old man up!"

Anchises, sister ship to the *Autolycus*. Standard 'A'-class ship which were the backbone of the revamped Blue Funnel fleet after the devastating losses during the 2nd World War.

The Times they are a'Changing!

The alteration of the clocks in the United Kingdom from Summer to Winter Time and vice versa every spring and autumn should have been plain sailing for everybody in the SeaSpeed flight crews to cope with. All of the SeaSpeed Hovercraft Commanders and flight crew were from a marine background and, as such, were more than used to alterations in the clocks. Virtually every night on the long sea passages when travelling in an easterly or westerly direction across the oceans of the world, the ship's clocks had to be altered backwards or forwards by 30 or even 60 minutes.

Part of our duties as Hovercraft Commanders was to arrive at the terminal in Cowes at least one hour before the first flight of the day to carry out a thorough daily inspection on the service craft and to sign for it and take over responsibility of it from the night Duty Engineer. This process took about 45 minutes and every function of the craft was inspected and tested before starting up, and then repositioning the craft to the apron (as the boarding area for the passengers was called) ready to load the first passengers of the day.

On one memorable occasion in the autumn, one of my colleagues arrived at the base at half past four, two whole hours before he was required to be there, much to the surprise of the night Duty Engineer who, having completed the servicing of the craft and carrying out routine maintenance as required, had settled down in his comfortable chair in the terminal building, nodded off, and was having forty winks. Much to the embarrassment of my colleague it then dawned upon everyone that instead of putting his clocks back one hour he had in fact advanced his clock one hour and was thus two hours ahead of, and totally out of sync with, everybody else! What also became apparent was that, as this occurred on a Monday morning, the nation's clocks having been put back to GMT 24 hours earlier on the Sunday at 2 o'clock in the morning, this colleague and his wife had spent the whole of the previous day 'out of sync' with everybody else. Poor chap took a long time to live that one down!

In the early-1970s, the 'powers that be' in Whitehall decided that instead of putting the clocks back to Greenwich Mean Time in the autumn they would leave the clocks on British Summer Time for the whole of the year. It meant that during the course of the winter, local time was out of sync with what the sun was doing. This rather silly experiment was tried for two consecutive years until everyone realised that you can't play with time zones and geography, and the idea was thankfully scrapped. One consequence during this experimental period of leaving the clocks as they were was that our first flight in the morning from Cowes at 0725 was in the dark, which required a flight crew of two Commanders; one as the Radar Operator, and one flying the craft. For safety reasons all flights in the hours of darkness were manned by two Commanders.

During the early years of hovering, the armed forces set up an 'Interservices Hovercraft Unit', based at HMS *Daedulus* on the shores at Lee-on-Solent, where the present-day Hovercraft Museum is now situated. This unit, known as the IHU, was set up for the three forces (Army, Navy and Air Force) to evaluate hovercraft generally, and was manned by various ranks of each individual service. Typical of any armed force, they had their own way of doing everything, and approached the whole concept of flying the machines in a somewhat unorthodox and (to us in the commercial world) very strange way.

My first encounter with these gentlemen of the IHU was while attending a one week Rolls Royce engine course at the Rolls Royce factory at Leavesden (now the Warner Brothers Film studios where the *Harry Potter* films were shot) with my two other SeaSpeed trainee Pilot colleagues to learn all about the workings of the 'Gnome' gas turbine. These highly sophisticated engines powered the SR.N5 and SR.N6 hovercraft that were prolific at that time, and which we were to learn to fly. It was necessary for us to attend this course and pass a fairly rigorous examination relating to the workings of the 'Gnome' gas turbine at the end of it before we were even allowed to sit in the driving seat of the craft and attempt to start the engine. One false move could do serious damage to the delicate workings of the 1,000 horse power gas turbine engine, so a week back 'in the classroom' was vital.

Also attending this course were three members of IHU: one Army Captain, an Army Staff Sergeant and a Royal Navy Lieutenant. The Army always, without fail, turned up late every morning to the classes, and had been furnished with 'instruction books' on how to handle, operate and fly the SR.N5 and SR.N6 craft that IHU operated. I won't go into the details of these manuals, but to liken them to the children's 'How it Works' Ladybird books of the day would not have been far off the mark! The manuals listed procedures by 'numbers' in typical military fashion, and one thing that one learned very quickly whilst training to fly these machines was that it was absolute 'seat of the pants' stuff. Of all the various ships and vehicles I handled throughout my career connected with the sea, the hovercraft was the vehicle that stood out from all the others as the one vehicle you simply could not ‘fly by numbers’. We also got the impression that these IHU chaps were somewhat aloof and lacked the enthusiasm that we had for the hovercraft – to them it seemed a duty rather than a privilege to be involved in this radical new method of transport.

Our primary concern when operating on all our routes was the safety of the passengers that we carried, and we had strict rules about negotiating the entrance to and departure from Cowes Harbour. The hovercraft channel that was laid out in Cowes Harbour and marked with little orange ‘pellet’ buoys was tight, mainly over mud flats at low water, clear of all the yachts moored on buoys in the open harbour, and there was a completely blind corner where we rounded the end of the eastern breakwater when the tide was at its lowest. Approaching from seaward to enter the harbour, there were the bright lights of the houses, buildings and the promenade of East Cowes to contend with, which rather distorted the view of the Commander actually flying the craft, so the help of the second Commander operating the radar was of vital importance.

One of our self-imposed regulations, adopted by most and eventually made regulatory by the Cowes Harbour Master, was that on approaching the hovercraft channel either outward or inward, we would broadcast a safety message by VHF radio on Channel 16 to the effect that we were about to enter/leave Cowes Harbour via the hovercraft channel and would be listening on VHF Channel 16. This would enable any other hovercraft in the area operating around that channel to make contact with us and avoid meeting at that blind corner with the associated risk of a collision.

It was not uncommon for one of the IHU craft to have been in Cowes overnight undergoing repairs at the British

Hovercraft Corporation's main factory, which was situated in East Cowes, and where the craft were built. After a night's revelry ashore on the island away from the prying eyes of their commanding officer at HMS *Daedulus*, they would return to their craft and leave Cowes at first light to return to their unit at Lee-on-Solent.

Of course, our friends in the services didn't consider this safety call on the VHF radio to be of any relevance to them, and they would carry on in their own sweet way regardless of anyone else in the area. On more than one occasion a near miss occurred when the regular scheduled passenger carrying hovercraft had met an IHU military craft at that blind corner, the latter being totally oblivious to all around it, and evasive action had to be taken very quickly, usually by the SeaSpeed craft.

At low water one morning during the aforementioned period of the experiment into not altering the clocks, I happened to be on duty flying the craft with a second Commander operating the radar. The first crossing from Cowes to Southampton was in darkness, but by 0800, on leaving Southampton to return to Cowes, there was usually enough light to see what was going on, and the Radar Operator could relax and either chat to the passengers or read his morning newspaper.

On approaching Cowes in the half light of early morning, I made the customary safety information broadcast announcing that Golf Hotel 2015 (the call sign for that hovercraft) was entering Cowes Harbour via the hovercraft channel and was listening on Channel 16. No response was detected – 'All quiet on the Western Front!' However, on approaching the harbour entrance, my colleague suddenly saw a yellow flashing light on the other side of the breakwater which, with it being low water, was making the notorious turn around the end of the breakwater completely blind. All hovercraft must display the usual lights as prescribed by the International Regulations for the Prevention of Collision at Sea – those pretty red, green and white lights one sees on all 'power driven vessels' on the water, but in addition hovercraft had to display, and indeed still do, an 'all round' flashing yellow light to identify themselves.

Departing Cowes for Southampton.

So, the conclusion that morning was that there was one of our military friends inside the harbour on his way out in his hovercraft, completely oblivious of us approaching at speed in the opposite direction with passengers on board. Immediately reducing speed and approaching extremely slowly, we lost sight of the flashing light as we got very close to the breakwater – our view of the inside of the harbour being completely obstructed. Repeated calls were made to the mystery 'hovercraft' and dropping our machine into the water and proceeding at very slow speed around the blind end of the breakwater peering for a visual contact with this mystery intruder, we then saw an Isle of Wight County Council dust cart slowly making its way along the East Cowes promenade emptying litter bins, complete with yellow flashing light on the roof of the vehicle's cab.

With much egg on our faces, I lifted the craft back on to the 'hover' and we made our way to the landing pad to disgorge our highly amused passengers into the terminal at Cowes. By the time I left on the next flight to Southampton, our 'hovering' dust cart had vanished into the side streets of East Cowes, hopefully never to confuse us again.

The 'Trincomalee Incident'

Homeward bound from the Far East on the *Ajax* after departing Penang, we were to make a scheduled stop to 'top off' with cargo in Trincomalee, Sri Lanka, and spirits were running high. The *Ajax* was blessed with a superb motor lifeboat, fitted with an unusually powerful 4-cylinder, water cooled, Thorneycroft diesel (rather than the more commonly fitted Petter air cooled variety), and that gave her a really good turn of speed.

Thoughts of beach parties and 'water skiing' on 'shit chutes' were on everybody's minds. In those terrible pre-conservation days, effluent from the toilets on board ship was simply 'dumped' over the side via internal piping, and when laid alongside in port, 'shit chutes' were dangled over the side to prevent effluent from landing directly onto the quay. These could be used as water skiing platforms towed behind the ship's motor lifeboat in suitable places, Trincomalee Harbour being probably the best place in the world for this activity! Then our wonderful 'chippy' (ship's carpenter) made this superb Mark 2a, hydro-dynamically designed, water skiing board/effluent diverter, which was tested at length earlier in the trip while anchored off Bangkok for two weeks awaiting berthing over the Christmas and New Year period of 1966/67.

We entered Trincomalee Harbour at dawn – the Pilot there was no fool, no night work for him – and passing through the heads and watching the vista of that great natural harbour open up always impressed everyone that had ever been there. We were alone in the harbour, save for one of the Dutch Royal Interocean Line's 6,000-ton Far

Eastern trading ships, the *Straat Colombo*, tied up on the only jetty man enough to take a ship that size. We, of course, were far too big, and proceeded to anchor in the stream.

Water 'skiing' antics on a shit chute towed behind the motor lifeboat!

Beach party.

Arriving on the stream mooring, as Third Officer and traditionally in charge of the motor lifeboat, I was delegated to seek the permission of the Master, Captain O'Hanlon, to launch the motor boat, and use it for transport to the beaches. I am pretty sure that 'Chrome Dome', as he was affectionately known, would have had a mutiny on his hands if he had refused, as there had been so much talk about it for so long that he knew what I was going to ask before I'd opened my mouth.

He had no objection whatsoever, providing that I took him round the ship every morning at 0900 to inspect the trim and see that the ship was looking smart – he could never resist interfering with what was basically the Chief Officer's job – in fact he couldn't help interfering in everybody's jobs, it was just the nature of the man. So, to humour him and keep him happy, at 0900 after he had finished his breakfast, there was the motor boat at the foot of the gangway every morning, having been launched, hosed out and cleaned by myself and the Senior Midshipman, who was expected to act as boat hand while I drove the Captain around the ship so that he could do his inspection. Idyllic days spent relaxing in glorious sunshine, with the cargo very slow to arrive from the shore, and seemingly no hurry to complete and rush away.

On the first night of our stay in Trincomalee, the predominantly 'Scouse' lads in the deck and catering departments were all very excited. Liverpool Football Club were doing really well in one of the European football competitions, and the lads were all staying up until God knows what time to listen to the match commentary on the BBC Overseas Service; Liverpool FC were in action against AFC Ajax of Amsterdam, and hopes were running high.

Next morning bodies were very scarce, but the motor boat

was at the gangway to take Captain O'Hanlon on his 'rounds' of the ship. Leaving the gangway, we proceeded towards the bows, pausing to check this and that, and then around the bows towards the stern. On rounding the stern, all hell broke loose, and I really thought that Chrome Dome's chromium dome was going to come off. On the stern were the proudly emblazoned letters of the ship's name, and under it, her port of registry. And someone had been fiddling about with a paint brush and a pot of white paint. After the ship's name, there was what appeared to be a squiggled 'S', and after the port of registry was a definite 'I'. Furious at this vandalism inflicted on his ship, he rounded on me and demanded to know what was going on. I honestly had not a clue, so I was ordered to return to the gangway, and summon the Chief Officer and Bosun to join us in the boat.

Alan Shoesmith, the Chief Officer, hurried down to the boat, and after a short delay the Bosun joined us as well. An avid Liverpool FC fan, the Bosun had sat up into the wee small hours with the rest, and in order to keep awake, had consumed his fair share of Tennent's lager, so he was feeling no pain at all. The solemn gathering was again transported to the stern of the ship, where Captain O'Hanlon demanded an explanation for this abomination that had befallen his smart ship.

Sitting in the boat, despite the heat of the early morning sun, an icy atmosphere prevailed, and blank stares at this addition to the names on the stern were suddenly replaced by a grin on the face of the Bosun. And when he explained that Liverpool had been soundly beaten in the first leg of their European match by the Dutch team Ajax by five goals to one, I am afraid that it was very hard to keep a straight face.

What had been added to the legend on the stern was:
AJAX 5 – LIVERPOOL 1

The offending graffiti.
Photo courtesy of the late Ted Milburn, Senior Radio Officer.

I am afraid that Captain O'Hanlon could not see the funny side of it at all, and later when I was required to take him to the jetty to board the *Straat Colombo* for what I remember as a very embarrassing interview with the Master of that ship, the Dutch Captain, although extremely polite and apologetic, was also obviously trying desperately to contain his amusement. It was obvious to one and all that some of the Dutch crew had also sat up to listen to their team beating Liverpool and, seeing a golden opportunity to take the mickey, had stolen across in the middle of the night, and added the score to the names on the stern of the *Ajax*, registered in Liverpool.

We met the Dutch lads at the beach that very afternoon and shared a glass or five with them – their Captain was with them and I will not forget the relaxed atmosphere amongst the crew. The Dutch Captain had tried to be as contrite as he could, but when we all thought about it, the whole incident became even more incredible.

What were the odds, we mused, of the two ships, one Dutch and the other British, being in port together, of Liverpool FC playing the Dutch football team Ajax that very night, and the British ship having the legend painted on her stern that just begged to be graffitied? When thinking about it even now, it brings a real smile to my mind.

The offending graffiti was expunged with a bit of black hull paint, and the affair came to an end, but it is one of those incidents that will always be a happy memory of those balmy days in idyllic foreign places.

North East by South, a Half West?

The fishing industry in Hull was devastated by the Cod Wars of the late '60s and '70s, and its decline was sad to watch. Thousands of people in the west of Hull around Hessle Road were affected and the way the industry tried to diversify was commendable, but there is only so much that can be done to alter a way of life that had existed for centuries.

The ways of the industry and life on a trawler were somewhat different to that on a merchant ship, and apart from the summer holidays I spent on trawlers while attending the local Nautical College in Hull for my pre-sea training before going to sea, I had little knowledge of the actual workings of the industry. This was fleshed out when I came more into contact with these fine hard-working men after becoming a Pilot on the Humber in 1975. I was aware that the Skippers and mates of the trawlers were qualified, as they studied for their examinations at the Fishermen's School which was part of the Nautical College. There was, however, a hard core of men who, although highly experienced and very knowledgeable, simply could not pass an exam to save their lives! These wonderful chaps were advanced to a rank known as 'Third Hand' – really an un-certificated officer below the rank of mate, who could keep a watch at sea, take responsibilities for running the trawler that he could easily cope with; he just didn't have that piece of paper that meant he could be signed on officially as the mate or Skipper of a trawler. They always seemed to be called 'Tommy' and would claim the privilege and honour of steering the trawler on the River Humber when she arrived from or sailed to the fishing grounds.

When a trawler arrived from the fishing grounds to unload its catch, the trawler would be formally handed back to the owners, together with a list of defects to be rectified during her short stay in port. Before she sailed again, she would be handed back to the Skipper following an inspection which entailed the generators being started (the ships were always on shore power whilst alongside in the dock) and every light, every searchlight, every bit of kit, every bit of navigational equipment and everything in the galleys and accommodation would be switched on to check it was working. On completion of this inspection, all the crew would be taken to the nearest pub for a drink (or several) by the owners. The generators on board would be shut down by the shore watchman, and the trawler would lay idle until the time came to sail for the fishing grounds. Two hours before sailing for the fishing grounds and the crew re-joined, the watchman would go down below into the engine room, start the generators and *everything* would come back on again, so the ship would literally burst back into life in a blaze of lights, and all the navigational equipment would slowly start to come back to life.

Such was the case one morning when I was rung at 0300 and issued with a piloting job to take the *St. Benedict*, a fairly modern stern fishing trawler out of Albert Dock in Hull to sea. The order included compass adjusting off the dock before proceeding to sea, but the Duty Pilot told me not to worry as this aspect of the operation wouldn't be taking place as there was dense fog throughout the river. On arrival at the ship, I made my way to the Skipper's cabin, where he was entertaining the owners to a farewell glass of 'lemonade' before we sailed. He said that, "Your colleague is already on board and up there in the wheelhouse," and I assumed he was referring to the compass adjusters. The adjusters were indeed in the wheelhouse, and greeted me with their customary, "Good morning Pilot – ta-ta Pilot!" indicating that they were well aware that no compass adjusting could take place due to the dense fog! It was then that I noticed another gentleman in similar uniform to mine making his way across the wheelhouse to greet me. Who was this I wondered? "Good morning Sir, are you the Humber Pilot?" to which I replied in the affirmative. "Oh good, pleased to meet you, I'm the North Sea Pilot"

Now this was a mystery – very large deep-drafted merchant vessels used to employ one of these North Sea Pilots when approaching the English Channel and the Dover Straits to help guide them through the relatively shallow waters of the North Sea to their destinations in Holland, Germany, the UK and further afield – their presence on board usually insisted upon by the ship's insurers for safety reasons. I'm talking here about super-tankers, very large bulk carriers and container ships of immense size, but a 'cod banger', as we affectionately called these comparatively small trawlers, this was something totally new. I then asked this Pilot where the ship was bound, to which he replied, "Falmouth." All suddenly became clear – that entailed going out of the Humber and turning *right* – 'Indian Territory' as far as the trawler men were concerned. Their usual trip to northern waters and the fishing grounds meant turning *left* after leaving the river, and they knew that route like the backs of their hands. This was something totally out of the ordinary for them and it transpired that they were bound south after mackerel in the western approaches off the coast of Cornwall. We chatted for a while before the Skipper appeared, and the North Sea Pilot mused that he had noticed a somewhat different approach to life on board the trawler: "They seem to do things a little differently on board here don't they?" to which I replied, "Oh yes, it's a whole new world for you I would imagine."

Once the Skipper arrived on the bridge, we had called the dock and made ready to leave the berth. We couldn't see across the dock due to the fog, and the fish dock tugs made fast but told me they couldn't accompany me through the lock into the river as they didn't have radar; not that this bothered me as I didn't really want them fast once in the tideway as it made life more difficult in the fog with tugs still attached. As long as they assisted us to line up for the lock, that would be fine and I wanted rid of them anyway. Just before letting go the ropes from the berth, 'Tommy', the Third Hand, appeared in the wheelhouse to take his honoured spot behind the wheel and assume his role of 'Tekking the ship to sea Pilot'. He was resplendent in his best suit and flat hat, but his collar was off, tie discarded, his teeth were out, and he had the customary roll-up of 'Old Friend' in his mouth – the trademark rolling tobacco of the fisherman of that era. I don't think the short stub of rolled cigarette was lit, it was just part of the uniform.

We left the berth, and for the whole manoeuvre I issued only orders to the tugs by radio, engine orders to the Skipper who was on the engine telegraph, and helm orders to 'Tommy' on the wheel by asking for rudder angles – no courses were requested at any time until we were clear of the lock and out into the river. For the greater part of the whole manoeuvre my head was stuck in the radar while we travelled down the dock, and once clear I lined her up for the river channel and only then did I ask Tommy, "How's your head?" meaning what compass heading was the ship on. Back came the answer, "East by north a quarter north, Pilot." In those days the usual way of reporting a heading or course was by the 360-degree notation – 090 for due east, 180 for due south, 270 for due west etc., but Tommy was of the 'old school' and had instantly looked at the magnetic compass and not the electric gyrocompass.

In those days electric gyrocompasses took some time to 'settle' and orientate themselves to register and display a true heading after being switched on, and as the power had only been restored to the compass after the watchman had restarted the ship's generators some two hours before, the gyrocompass was still settling down. So the old system of magnetic compass and the ancient way of denoting courses would have to be used for the passage. Fortunately, in those 'ancient' days, one of the required certificates that I had to obtain as part of my apprenticeship at sea with Alfred Holt's Blue Funnel Line was a Lifeboatman's Certificate. Part of that course was learning to 'box the compass' by 'quarter points' – an archaic system used back through time immemorial on sailing ships in Nelson's day and beyond, but thank heavens I had learnt it and could remember it off by heart. As part of that Lifeboatman's Certificate Exam we had to 'box the compass' in quarter points out loud to the examiner, sometimes backwards for example from east to north, and woe betide us if we got it wrong.

So, when Tommy reported the course in the old quarter point system of compass headings, I simply carried on. We continued down the channel, following the gentle curve of the river and altering course slowly and progressively, past the docks in Hull and then the tanker jetties at Saltend until heading down Halton Middle towards Immingham, all done in 'quarter points'. The Skipper then suddenly exclaimed, "Oh look Pilot, I can see the next float," and after having my head stuck in the radar for some time, I looked up to be able to make visual contact with those little blips on the radar screen I had been following. Stretching my spine straight I revelled in the temporary clearance of the fog and was able to relax a little, at least for a while until the fog descended once again.

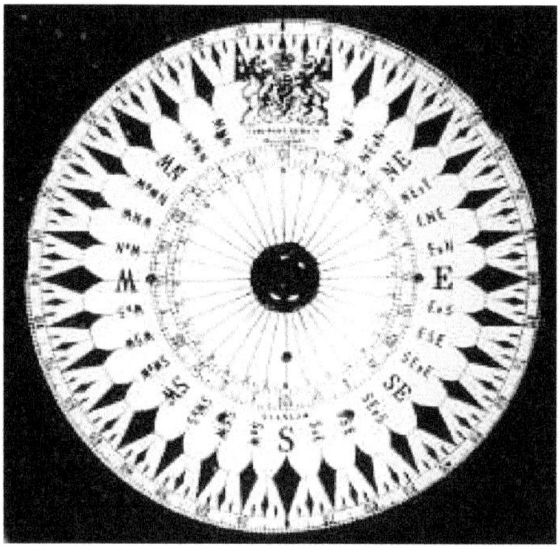

Compass rose with quarter points.

Whilst wandering about I noticed my North Sea Pilot colleague deep in concentration over a small grubby piece of paper on which he was frantically scribbling. The Skipper had also noticed and asked me quietly what I thought he was doing. After a moment's thought, the penny dropped – obviously he had assumed that they did everything in quarter points on the ship and he was rapidly converting his 360-degree notation courses into quarter point courses. In fact, seeing me relieved of the intensive concentration of conning the ship by radar he sidled over to me and quietly asked, "Do they do everything in quarter points on here?" I'm afraid I rather mischievously replied, "Yes," at which point he dived back to his bit of grubby paper with a strained look on his face and continued his hasty calculations. I didn't leave him in his misery for long though and I went to him and explained that by the time we got to Spurn and cleared the river into the open sea, the gyrocompass would have settled down and the automatic pilot would be able to be used. The relief on his face was an absolute picture even in the half light of the wheelhouse on that foggy morning, and I often wondered afterwards how he got on with the lads during the passage round to Falmouth.

St. Benedict.

The demise of the fishing industry was painful to watch with so many fine hard-working people thrown out of work and a way of life coming abruptly to an end. Yes, the industry diversified, but never really recovered. Icelandic trawlers eventually started to come to Hull to land their catches, and I did Pilot several of them up to the dock when they arrived. I remember one very cocky crew on one of them asking me where the best pubs were on the shore as they wanted to go ashore and boast their good luck at defeating the mighty

English fishermen. I'm afraid I was rather curt with my reply and advised them of two things. Firstly, I counselled that before we arrived at the dock, they would be best advised to take down their Icelandic flag and either display a Norwegian ensign or not bother to fly one at all. Secondly, if they were intent on venturing ashore, it would probably be better if they identified themselves as Norwegians or Faroe Islanders. Mystified they asked why? I merely said that they should be aware of the consequences of their government's actions in the Cod Wars, and the utter devastating effect they, as Icelanders, had caused to the community ashore in Hull. I made it quite clear that I was therefore worried for their safety ashore.

The rest of that particular passage up the river was conducted in a somewhat more sombre mood.

Tales of the Old Harbour

To some of us, the 'Old Harbour', or to name it properly, the River Hull gave us nightmares. The river at Kingston upon Hull is the River Hull, which rises in the Yorkshire Wolds and flows into the River Humber where the city is situated on the banks of the mighty Humber Estuary. The city of Hull had its name changed from Wyke on Hull to Kingston (Kings Town) upon Hull during the reign of Edward the First in 1299, when Edward took over the port and gave it a Royal Charter. Its original name of Wyke came from the Scandinavian word 'vik' meaning a creek, and to us Pilots, that is exactly what it was; a muddy creek! The original port of Hull was in fact this river, or The Old Harbour as it was known, long before any of the present-day docks were formed.

To a true 'Kingstonian' the name simply used as Hull or 'Ull is abhorrent, and I am proud to be a Kingstonian from Kingston upon Hull rather than some of the other less auspicious nomenclatures given to us.

However, the Old Harbour does have significance to the Humber Pilot Service (as was before 2002) because it was Henry the Eighth who, in 1541, on observing a 'foreign' (Scottish) ship trying and failing to enter the River Hull, commanded one of the elder brethren of Hull Trinity House to go off in a boat to board and conduct the ship safely into the river. As the elder brother succeeded at the first attempt, impressing Henry the Eighth, His Majesty granted the elder brethren a Royal Charter confirming the foundation of the Humber Pilot Service. The motto *Semper Paratus* – Always Ready – was true to the last day of that fine service of which I was proud to be a part for 27 years.

But I'm afraid that this Royal Charter did not exempt us from the nightmares that bugged us about the entry to the River Hull. On a good day it could be a bit of a problem to get it absolutely right, and most entries to it were more good luck than good management. And what went on up there was even more of a problem. The original Harbour Master when I started as a Pilot was too amenable to the wishes of the barge Skippers who seemed to rule the roost and do what they liked. They littered the harbour with their charges and gave little or no thought to the problems we, as Pilots, had in bringing the ships into the River Hull. Often, it was virtually impossible to weave the ships through the narrow gaps left by the barges, and we had great difficulty finding enough room to swing the ships prior to them proceeding further up the river under the charge of the redoubtable Bankses, the father and son team of Old Harbour Pilots who took the ships on up the river to their berths after we had brought them in from the Humber.

The limits of our 'district' and our jurisdiction ended at North Bridge, where we would hand over the ship to the Bankses before it went further on up the river. On one occasion when the Harbour Master went on leave, the senior member of the Banks family ('Old Tom') stood in for the him, and when a barge started to tie up actually in the channel for the ships, thus blocking it almost completely, Old Tom told him to move it. When the barge Skipper challenged his right to tell him to 'move it', Old Tom indicated with a threateningly clenched fist to the barge Skipper exactly what authority he had to tell him to move the barge! The barge was moved rather quickly.

The entry to the river from the Humber could be fraught with difficulty. To get a ship in successfully it had to be manoeuvred in very close to the North Bank alongside what was Victoria Pier and the Horsewash. The Horsewash was an old slipway where the dray horses that pulled the wagons in days gone by would be allowed to wallow in the waters of the River Humber to cool off their hooves, and the slip is still used today for recreational purposes, long after the horses have gone. The current in the Humber is very strong and flows relentlessly up the river until almost high tide at Hull, and the current into the River Hull is equally strong at its entrance but running in a totally different direction to that in the main estuary. So, when entering the Old Harbour the positioning of the ship is crucial, and if you don't get it quite right it leads to some heart-stopping moments with visions of ending up straddled across the entrance to the river, ship's bow aground on Sammy's Point to the east, and the stern hard alongside the stone wall and the mud of the west side of the river entrance. One of my overzealous and foolhardy colleagues once tried to enter without using the time-honoured method and ended up aground for a complete tide in that embarrassing position. I didn't actually see it as I was on leave at the time, but others told me afterwards that at low water one could have walked under the middle of the ship as it was high and dry bridging the gap, the bow and stern firmly aground!

The depth of water in the reaches further up the River Hull were a mystery to us, and the ships relied on the knowledge of Old Tom Banks to guide them up there safely. In the 1960s, before the advent of VHF radio communication being regularly fitted to all ships, one of my late colleagues, 'Tuffy' Brownlow, was boarded on an old German coaster from the Sea Station Pilot cutter outside the entrance to the Humber, and the ship was bound for the River Hull with a cargo of seed for crushing and processing at the British

Extracting Company's Mill. Not having any direct contact with Hull Radio, the port control of the day, and going only on the word of the Master, Tuffy proceeded up to the entrance of the River Hull and entered the river at the appropriate time. Once in the River Hull, he turned the ship in the swinging basin, and 'blew' for Drypool Bridge to be opened for him. This entailed giving three blasts on the ship's whistle which, when heard by the bridge operator, would result in the bridge being lifted to allow the ship to pass through. The manoeuvre by this time was with the ship proceeding stern first (backwards) and was another test of ship handling expertise as ships don't go backwards in a straight line like a car and they need some coaxing. On passing through Drypool Bridge, Tuffy tied the ship up against some barges for her to wait for Tom Banks to arrive, as the next bridge was North Bridge where our jurisdiction as Humber Pilots ran out. The Master hospitably offered Tuffy a beer before he left and, after downing the drink, Tuffy departed to walk back to the Pilot Office in Hull, stopping off at the Harbour Master's office on the way to enquire where the River Hull Pilot was.

There was no sign of the Harbour Master, which Tuffy thought a little unusual but not surprising as the Harbour Master wasn't one to hang around once ships had passed his office situated at Drypool Bridge. By now it was getting a little late on the 'tide', so Tuffy went back to the ship to advise the Master of the absence of his Pilot. The Master then said to Tuffy, "Well can you take me up there?" Tuffy replied by pointing out that our jurisdiction ended where the ship was temporarily berthed, and the last time Tuffy had been up above North Bridge was in a canoe when he was 14! His berth was a further one mile up the river and Tuffy didn't know what the depths were or whether there would be anybody there to meet them – the Banks usually providing rope handling duties as well as piloting the ships.

The Master then offered to make it worth Tuffy's while if he helped him and, after another beer, Tuffy agreed to have a go. He 'blew' for North Bridge which obligingly opened for him, and then proceeded to do the same at Scott Street Bridge, Chapman Street Bridge, and the Railway Bridge at Wilmington, all of which the ship passed through comfortably plodding backwards towards its berth. On arrival off the berth, Tuffy came at last unstuck and his luck ran out, running firmly aground and not being able to move. A passing barge was 'roped in' to help, and with the fee of a bottle of German brandy, the barge Skipper cheerfully assisted and pushed the ship alongside the mill at British Extracting. Highly delighted, the Master then dropped a sizeable cash fee into Tuffy's hands, plied him with more beer, and then Tuffy took his leave to walk back to the Pilot Office.

On arrival back at the office, he picked up the intercom phone to Hull Radio, which was situated on the fourth floor of the Pilot Office at the pier, and informed them that the ship he had brought up was on her berth at the British Extracting Company's Mill. "Oh, that's funny," replied the operator. "As you know Tuffy, the tide today is a small neap tide and not a big spring tide, so there's not enough water in the river for her to get to her berth and she's going up the day after tomorrow!"

More Tales of the Old Harbour

There are many tales of the Old Harbour – the River Hull – which was originally the port of Hull. As mentioned in a previous tale we all had stories of funny goings on up there, and there are many, a couple of which are related here.

The lifting bridges at Drypool, North and all subsequent bridges further up the river could be lifted or swung on demand from the ships approaching by the sounding of the ship's whistle or hooter three times in quick succession. The bridge operator would then close the barriers to prevent road and pedestrian traffic crossing and open the bridge to river traffic. The sounding of the ship's whistle or horn would reverberate around the buildings that were situated on the banks of the river, old former mills and disused warehouses from the days when the Old Harbour was in full swing. In the 1970s some of these old buildings were renovated and converted into posh 'downtown' apartments for the more affluent, but the residents at one point rather tetchily wrote to the River Hull Harbour Master and the Pilotage Operations Manager demanding that these noisy interruptions to their beauty sleep must cease forthwith. I'm afraid that the reaction of Pilots was to actually continue, and in some cases for a short period, repeat the whistle signals requesting the bridge to open! The Pilotage Operations Manager was not one to suffer fools gladly, and his curt reply to the residents of these apartments was that if they chose to live close to a working river, they would have to accept the noises that went with that residency! I suppose it was a similar scenario to those nouveau riche village 'incomers' who demand that village church bells should be silenced as it disturbs their new-found countryside peace!

Similarly, in the main River Humber, when a ship was to be swung around in a short manoeuvre to face the incoming current before commencing a berthing or docking manoeuvre, a signal was sounded consisting of four short blasts followed by one long blast (if turning to starboard) and the residents of the new Victoria Dock Estate issued a similar demand for quiet from the ships. This was also replied to in a similar manner, and many Pilots who had not bothered with this signal, rather had announced their intentions over the VHF radio, also chimed in with this sound signal.

The actual workings of the lifting bridges in the Old Harbour was a very simple mechanism. Known as a 'Scherzer Rolling Bascule Bridge', the bridges have a 'balancing water tank' one side of their curved section that counterbalanced the enormous weight of the bridge when it was being raised. The actual lifting of the bridge was achieved by a rack and pinion system that was driven by electric motors, and the bridge span simply rolled on the curved section of its structure. The lifting was a very graceful sight to watch and achieved in a couple of minutes before the ship backed through on its way up the river to its berth.

On one occasion Drypool Bridge suffered a rather catastrophic mechanical failure due to wear and tear, and the guts of the rack and pinion system had to be removed for repairs, stranding a couple of small coasters that were above the bridge at their berths. In order to lift the bridge, a very large mobile crane was sited on the east side of the river, where the opening part of the bridge landed when down, and this crane was then used to substitute the lifting action and river traffic could carry on while repairs were carried out. The crane attached wire slings to the body of the bridge and simply lifted it up and held it in the raised position while the ship passed through. It was a very temporary system which worked, but like any temporary system it had its dangers, and we as Pilots used to wait until the bridge was all the way up and locked in its raised position before attempting to pass beneath this enormous structure held rather precariously in the sky.

While these repairs were ongoing, I was given a small British coaster belonging to Crescent Shipping – the 'cup o' tea boats' as we used to call them – and she was bound for a berth upstream of Drypool Bridge during this breakdown period. I had turned her around and was waiting for the bridge to be opened at a berth literally 50 feet from the bridge, ready to back through once the bridge was lifted. Once the crane had been positioned the lift commenced, and when up, the Harbour Master who was superintending the operation assured me that the locking pins on the bridge were 'in' and I could proceed. I was doubtful as the bridge still seemed to be lifting but took his word for it and I started to back the ship into the bridge hole. There was then an ominous sound indicating that the wire slings attached to the bridge were starting to fail, and on looking up I saw that they had indeed snapped and the bridge was on its way down – rather quickly. I shouted to the Captain of the coaster to put the engines full ahead, and as we shot back out of the bridge hole the accommodation and wheelhouse of the ship just escaped being crushed by the descending mass of steel. What didn't quite escape was the ship's ensign flag pole right at the extreme after end of the ship which was spilt into several pieces from top to bottom, a very lucky escape from what could have been a rather nasty outcome.

The bridge, after landing with a very loud bang, 'bounced' on its seating for some time, fetching car drivers who were waiting to cross the river from their cars to see what was going on. One of these drivers turned out to be my godmother who was actually first in the queue to cross, and who was understandably slightly miffed at being caught by the bridge opening, delaying her trip home from work! When she saw it was me, she just laughed and said what strange goings on occurred on the river!

Drypool Bridge open to allow a ship to pass through.

That episode was rather embarrassing to me personally as I had a long-standing fellow ship's officer friend from years before staying with me at the time, and I had invited him to accompany me on the river to see what I did for a living. He has never forgotten that incident and frequently rather wryly asked me afterwards whether any bridges had dropped on me recently!

Another large construction that was introduced to the infrastructure of the City of Kingston upon Hull was the Tidal Surge Barrier. The city was very prone to flooding and in the 1950s, as a 'cherubic' choirboy in our local parish church in Kirk Ella, I can remember exchanging with the choir of St Mary's Parish Church in the Old Town. On occasion while singing there, the doors of the church would burst open during the service and the river water would flow down the aisle. Trousers rolled up, shoes off and hems of cassocks raised we would recess at the conclusion of the service and then dry off in the vestry prior to going home!

Many attempts were made to stem this devastation in large parts of the city, but it was not until the Tidal Surge Barrier was built during the 1970s that the flooding was alleviated and businesses and properties in the city could relax! The 'guillotine' style structure took some time to complete, and it was during the build process that we had quite a lot of fun navigating through a very much reduced aperture that had to be created. A concrete sill had to be built across the bed of the river for the bottom of the gate to sit on when closed and, in order to achieve this, a watertight enclosure was built across half of the river so that the concrete could be poured and the sill constructed. On the rising tide, when entering the river with a ship, the following current was very strong, and halving the width of the river at the site created a marked downhill slide which made matters somewhat more difficult to handle!

To add to these problems, there was a berth just upstream of this new hazard which was dedicated to petrol and oil barges that plied their trade on the Humber, Ouse and Trent, travelling many miles into the heartlands of Yorkshire and Nottinghamshire carrying their potentially lethal and explosive cargoes from ports on the Humber to storage depots far afield. These empty barges sat on this berth when not being used, full of explosive petroleum gas and in a far more dangerous state than when they were full, so that when we ran the gauntlet of this 'river rapid' created by halving the width of the river, we were presented with a gaggle of these potential time bombs ready to cause an almighty bang should we collide with them. Our reaction was to ban night time dark entries into the river for safety's sake, which was widely accepted as being prudent.

I boarded a small German coaster one day for his entry to the Old Harbour, and the Master politely enquired as to why he had been held back from going up the previous night time tide. When I explained he readily accepted the reason but countered that he had a stern anchor – something that we were not used to seeing or using – and that he used it all the time on the River Rhine for entering the small harbours that existed along the banks of that mighty German waterway. "You tell me when you want to stop Pilot," said the Captain, "and I'll demonstrate." Sure enough, at the appropriate moment when we had negotiated this 'downhill slalom' careering through the narrow hole, I yelled, and the Captain stopped the ship in an absolute straight line completely under control without the cursed swing that a ship suffers when going astern on its engines. I was very impressed and told him so as I had never seen it done before.

When completed, the surge barrier was a very impressive sight to behold, and once additional flooding protection was added around the banks of the River Hull adjacent to the streets of the Old Town, it helped to stop the flooding that had plagued residents for years. Its operation was very simple – it was a guillotine that chopped off the supply of the excessive height of tide in the River Humber from the River Hull, holding it back by coming down vertically into the swirling waters. When raised it was stowed in a horizontal position at the top of the barrier towers, swinging through 90 degrees when being lowered to nestle in its side slides and the concrete sill across the bed of the river, forming a watertight seal. Of necessity it was immensely strong and was built with large external steel 'webs' to stiffen it.

Tidal Surge Barrier, open. Photo courtesy of Dr S. McLelland.

Tidal Surge Barrier closing.
Photo courtesy of Terry Carrott/Yorkshire Post.

Tidal Surge Barrier closed.
Photo courtesy of Professor Tom Coulthard.

On one occasion a rather impatient colleague of mine – John Warboys – was issued with a job to take a ship away from the Old Harbour and out to sea, and on arrival at the ship saw that the surge barrier was closed due to an impending very high tide with a tidal surge on top of it, destined to flow into the Old Town streets and cause flooding. He bemoaned the delay to the Harbour Master, who told him that there was nothing that could be done as the barrier was under the control of the Yorkshire Water Authority and nothing to do with him.

Slightly peeved, John, always keen to get finished as soon as possible, asked the Captain of his ship to let go from the berth, and they proceeded down the river towards the site of the barrier to await its opening. As they approached, the warning sirens went off, indicating that the barrier was about to be lifted, so John carried on getting precariously close to the barrier itself, which was now being slowly lifted from the river bed. John, it being a lovely summer's day, had his jacket off and was standing out on the ship's bridge wing in his shirt sleeves conning the ship and issuing instructions to the Captain.

When there was barely enough clearance under the bottom of the lifting guillotine gate itself, the ever-impetuous John edged the foremast of the ship under the gate and took the ship's accommodation and wheelhouse even closer. However, as the ship came very close to touching the still rising gate, the gate itself started to rotate through its 90-degree turn to take up its horizontal stowed position. Seeing that he was going to have enough clearance under the rising gate, John asked for an 'ahead' movement of the ship's engines and started to actually creep under the now levelling off gate. What happened next was chaos! As the gate rotated and levelled off, all the water and river mud that was trapped in the steel webs that stiffen the structure of the gate dropped off onto the ship's bridge and accommodation, soaking John who was outside the shelter of the wheelhouse. Being the total professional, John stayed at his post conning the ship from outside and issuing instructions to the Captain, who had collapsed with laughter in the dry inside of the wheelhouse. He apparently was barely able to contain his mirth while John stoically remained at his post taking the ship safely out into the River Humber to continue her passage out to sea.

When John arrived at the mouth of the river to be taken off onto the Pilot launch, there was a brief delay, which the Captain of the ship excused by saying that the Pilot was getting dressed again. When John climbed off onto the launch, he was immediately quizzed by his other colleagues already on the launch as to what had gone on, his clothes now almost dry but still stinking somewhat of River Hull mud and detritus. The Captain of the ship, after obeying John's instructions for wheel and engine movements to clear the Old Harbour, had eventually got over his amusement and stopped laughing at what had happened. He had very kindly loaned John some floppy loose clothes while another member of the crew had taken his wet uniform shirt and trousers down into the warmest part of the engine room to hang on railings and dry off prior to John's departure on reaching the sea some two hours later.

Ever the pragmatist with a devil may care attitude, John appreciated the funny side of the incident, but never admitted that what he had done was unusual. The rest of the service however lived for a long time on relating that funny story to others!

Orfft We Jolly Well Go Then

One of the little things we used to do before setting off on a flight across the Solent, either from Cowes or Southampton, was to make a short 'Welcome Aboard' announcement over the Tannoy system before taking off, briefly describing the weather 'out there on the briny' and give an approximate passage time to the destination. This was done mainly to reaffirm our close relationship with our regulars, and also to put at ease those who may have never travelled on a hovercraft before. Quite often the weather was a little 'inclement' and if we were going to take a roundabout route to make the passage more comfortable for the passengers, then we would also briefly mention this – again to reassure and to calm the nerves of those who had not experienced the unique capability of the hovercraft to transfer from one surface to another without any fuss or bother whatsoever – be it from land to water or vice versa.

Anyone who had not experienced this before could show alarm travelling over water at maybe 40 or 50 knots and approaching a spit of land with no water over it. It was not uncommon to detect little gasps from passengers as you transited seamlessly from water to land then back to water with all the ease in the world. The straight-line route we took from Cowes to Southampton crossed many completely dry patches as we purposely kept well clear of the busy shipping lanes and conventional ferry routes in order to increase safety and make the passage times as quick as possible.

One of the many reasons that the 38-seat SR.N6 was 'stretched' was to accommodate more passengers and enable us to carry 56 passengers, which was the size in those days of a standard coach, and one of the regular charters that we used to undertake in the summer was what was affectionately known as the 'Midland Red Specials'. These special trips for 56 unsuspecting residents of Birmingham would start at about 6.30am in Birmingham on a Midland Red coach that would transport them to our Southampton terminal where we would be waiting with an empty SR.N6 Mark 1S hovercraft, ready to take them to the Isle of Wight for a day out. One has to remember that in those days, motorways were in their relative infancy, and the journey south was tortuous to say the least.

On arrival at the hovercraft terminal the coach would disgorge its passengers and our Beach Master would usher the passengers onto the empty craft sitting high and dry on the apron in front of the terminal building. Some of them would of course require to use the loo before boarding, and we would wait until they had all boarded before proceeding out to the craft to start the engine and get under way. On sale at all hovercraft terminals in those days was a range of memorabilia, and one of the best sellers was the Ladybird book *How the Hovercraft Works*, a child's introduction to the practical theory and some of the slightly more technical details of operations of hovercraft of the day.

As a way to 'reassure' the anxious sea of faces that we were presented with when we inserted ourselves into the Pilot's seat at the front of the passenger cabin of the craft, we would often solemnly take one of these children's books out with us and, in full view of these day trippers, prop it up on the console in front of us, seemingly scanning the pages for some tips on how to drive this strange beast that many of them had never seen before. Strange mutterings, some slightly tinged with alarm would then start emanating from behind us, and before it got to mutinous levels, we would make the 'Welcome Aboard' announcement, and start winding up the Gnome gas turbine engine prior to taking off. We would of course then assure the passengers that we had done this 'once or twice before' and hopefully this would bring them back to reality and make them realise they were, in fact, in perfectly safe hands. If conditions allowed during the crossing, we would try to give a light-hearted running commentary, pointing out some places of interest on the route, and tell them a bit about the craft they were travelling in. They were, after all, pleasure seekers who were out for a day trip, and we would endeavour to make their trip a memorable and happy one.

On arrival at Cowes, they would be ushered aboard an Isle of Wight bus company 'Vectis' coach which would take them on their round the island excursion, and this would return them to our Cowes terminal about 1800 for their return trip to re-join their Midland Red coach which would take them back to Birmingham. A full day out for these dedicated landlubbers from the very centre of the UK mainland, some of whom may have never been to sea before, and almost certainly had never seen a hovercraft, let alone experienced travelling on one. Certainly, we would receive letters of thanks from some of these people at a later date, occasionally mentioning the shock and horror of seeing the Hovercraft Commander referring to a Ladybird book of *How the Hovercraft Worked* before taking off. 'Brummies' have a great sense of humour, and some of the comments we received were indicative of their sense of excitement at riding in one of those fabulous machines.

We carried out many 'special' trips, which were introduced over many years by the various Route Managers we had during my time with SeaSpeed. Some of those Route Managers were extremely 'go ahead', and some were of the archetypical 'British Railways' genre, not necessarily forward looking or streetwise and definitely not very imaginative. Because these craft didn't run on rails, and the excuse of 'leaves on the line' couldn't be used to explain away delays (usually caused by strong winds and high seas) then a lot of them were somewhat stumped when it came to public relations.

One such manager in the early days was a thoroughly nice chap with sadly little or no sense of humour. He took a dim view one morning when one of the more senior Commanders added after his short pre-flight chat over the intercom that lovely little phrase coined by the late, great, Radio 2 DJ, Jimmy Young: "Orfft we jolly well go then!" I'm afraid that the Commander was reprimanded by our rather unimaginative and staid manager for that, the excuse for the roasting being that the Commander wasn't taking the job seriously enough.

That same manager, however, was open to suggestions to provide additional services for the residents of the Isle of Wight, and the germ of an idea and indeed the start of some of the more memorable 'specials' that we did came from one of the young ladies we affectionately called the 'hens', our hard-working dedicated terminal girls who sold tickets and generally looked after the passengers before they went out to board the craft. The life for young people on the island in the 1970s was starved of any appropriate culture for them; no pop stars or concerts ever came to the island and the social life was very limited. If you didn't sail, walk the dogs or horse ride you were stumped! And yet just across that stretch of water on the mainland it was 'all happening'.

It was one of the 'hens', Jenny, who came up with the idea of running a late-night special to Southampton, providing the younger generation of the island with an opportunity to see a major pop group at one of the many theatres in the big city, and then returning them late at night to the island. The manager picked up on this straight away, and after a brief meeting with us as to availability and willingness of Commanders to run such a special, checking that the SeaSpeed bus would also be available to take the theatre goers from the terminal to the The Gaumont, marketing and advertising of the special trip started in earnest. That very first 'special' was to see Emerson, Lake and Palmer at the The Gaumont, and was an instant sell out, the craft being filled within 24 hours of it being advertised. Jenny checked with the manager and suggested that she travel to the theatre to get the tickets there and then, but British Rail protocol deemed that only the manager could make such purchases involving a relatively large amount of cash, so it was left to him.

Two days before the special was to be run, the girls at the terminal asked for the tickets to be brought to the Cowes Terminal so they could start packing up the itinerary into envelopes for each individual passenger that had booked for the trip, and the manager said he would go across to Southampton to bring the tickets back. Then the bombshell! He hadn't actually booked the tickets at all, just assumed he could breeze into the box office and get them from the theatre a couple of days before the actual performance. Shock horror – 56 very disappointed concert goers, including Jenny herself and a couple of the other terminal staff who were itching for that bit of the high life that was sadly denied to them because of living on the island! The tickets for the performance had been sold out by the theatre in Southampton within 24 hours of them going on sale.

There was of course much egg on the manager's face, and

after that the organising and purchasing of tickets for any special was done by the hens themselves in conjunction with the Commanders, the Beach Masters and anyone within the organisation who was keen to see some of the marvellous shows that came to the mainland on a regular basis. I personally remember seeing Victor Borge on tour, there were many trips to see productions of major plays, West End shows on tour, the ballet came to town regularly, and we benefited the populace of the island with as many trips as we could arrange for them. Keeping in mind the younger generation, there were specials to see the Kinks, the Stones, Queen and many other famous pop groups of the time. Tickets were purchased well before any advertising was done, and the trips became a regular feature of island life.

However, I'll never forget Emerson, Lake and Palmer, who incidentally, sadly, never returned to perform in Southampton.

On the pad at Southampton.

The Navy Lark

One of the things a Pilot would dread was to be told when being issued with a job that you had a Royal Navy ship. I can remember having these fine ships kicked around by every Pilot trying to rid himself of the mild curse that was these 'Grey Funnel' ships, owned by Her Majesty the Queen and run in such strange and alien ways to those known and practised by professional Merchant Navy Captains and officers who had become Pilots.

The Royal Navy had their own unique way of doing things, and although I am sure that during war time there were the necessary ways of going about things, they were totally and sometimes incomprehensibly at odds with the way the 'proper (Merchant) Navy' did things! Terminology was strange, their ship-handling methods were peculiar, but they seemed to get away with it, much to our annoyance as Pilots. I was once asked by a non-marine friend what exactly I did for a living, and I replied with some caution that I regarded myself as a professional and experienced ship handler with intimate local knowledge. As an aside, I then recalled that I had, only two nights earlier, been hauled unceremoniously into position on to the berth at Barrow Clay Pits – a long since, thankfully defunct, and abandoned 'ocean terminal' – or to be more accurate a 'hole in the bank' on the south side of the Humber. The 'hauling' had been carried out by a 40-ton Volvo dump truck, after I had made a somewhat abortive approach to the berth and ran out of water!

Back to the Navy. Even though they seemed to go about things in a totally different way, they nonetheless generally got away with it and if they crashed and bent their ships, well it was a popularly held belief that they were promoted so they couldn't do it again. When one was boarded on a Royal Navy ship, more often than not one was greeted formally and politely, and then informed that the 'Navigating Officer' would be taking the ship up the river, and you were shepherded into a corner and initially ignored. However, it wouldn't be long on a river as busy as the Humber before the Navigating Officer would be asking for a bit of help and advice, and things would get better and one would feel a little more appreciated. Frequently, the officers on a naval vessel couldn't get over the volume of traffic that prevailed on the Humber, and timely avoiding action was sometimes required by their Pilot to prevent accidents. They couldn't get used to the strength of the tidal current and could totally misjudge it or fail to allow for it when setting courses up the relatively narrow channels. Approaching a berth or a lock, the Captain would politely inform his Pilot that he would be handling and docking the ship – that was until he got into bother, misjudged the strength of the current and was about to create some headlines in the local press. Given the use of tugs he would back away fairly quickly; tugs were alien to the Royal Navy whereas we Pilots used them as tools to great effect and advantage.

I think one of the main problems we had with them was getting used to the sheer volume of bodies that would be in the wheelhouse on any approach to a dock or berth. People would appear from nowhere, and the small confines of a wheelhouse would suddenly become packed with people giving out – to us – what seemed totally unnecessary information that led to total confusion. The depth of water 50 metres out to starboard and to port continually being relayed was a prime example. As a ship handler in shallow waters you don't give a monkeys what the depth is 50 metres away from the ship, just the amount of water that was under the ship where you actually were would have been nice!

When HRH Prince Charles joined the Royal Navy, and was subsequently in 1976 given command of HMS *Bronington*, there was a panic in Hull Roads when she appeared to pick up a Pilot to take her to Goole. HRH had declined the services of a Lower Station Pilot, as was his right, and on advice from the Pilot Station at Spurn, had arrived in Hull Roads at the required time. None of the Goole Pilots particularly wanted to take the responsibility, or the risk of running aground with such an esteemed Captain in charge. Eventually it was sorted out and one of the senior Pilots took the *Bronington* up to Goole without incident, and berthed her.

The Royal Yacht *Britannia* came to the river during Her Majesty the Queen's Silver Jubilee celebrations in 1977, and in deference to Her Majesty, the senior Lower Station Humber Pilot was despatched to board the yacht in Newcastle where the Queen had been making a visit prior to her coming to the Humber. There were two reasons for this: firstly, the most senior man was delegated to the job to avoid any 'jiggling about' when the yacht arrived off the river; and secondly, the Admirals in charge of the yacht (of which there were three on board) didn't want our dirty Pilot launches going alongside their pride and joy to board a Pilot at sea – the launch may dirty, or worse still, scratch the immaculate paintwork of the hull of the *Britannia*. When the Royal Yacht departed the river and the Pilot had to be taken off, they lowered one of their own boats to waterline level and the Pilot disembarked from her to our grotty launch.

Our senior Pilot at the time was someone who didn't suffer fools gladly, and he was extremely reticent to talk about what went on whilst on the bridge of the *Britannia* – all we gathered was that it had been a somewhat testing time for him, and his patience!

Taking the Pilot off the Royal Yacht *Britannia*.

Our patience was sometimes tested to the limit, and I recall one incident where I was boarded on HMS *Wilton*, the first minesweeper of the 1970s with a fibreglass hull. She carried the flotilla leader of a small group of these minesweepers that were assembling in Grimsby to carry out manoeuvres in the North Sea, and the other ships of the flotilla that were already in Grimsby awaiting the *Wilton*'s arrival were apparently not looking forward to having their Flotilla Commander joining them. My brother had taken one of the other minesweepers into Grimsby on a previous tide and had been told of this, so he warned me that the job, although on the face of it a relatively easy one, could be fraught with problems. Indeed, that turned out to be the case, with the Flotilla Commander insisting that he would handle his ship, and making a rather untidy job of it. In those pre-Humber Bridge days, travel from Grimsby back to Hull was a tortuous and drawn-out procedure – train from Grimsby Dock Station to New Holland, and then ferry to Hull – if the tide allowed.

After much performing in the dock attempting to get alongside the jetty, this Captain ended up flat alongside a tug laying on the dock wall on the opposite side of the dock to his berth, with ropes out from bow and stern across the dock to his berth, but trapping the tug in between his ship and the dock wall. He then requested that this tug 'help him' by pushing him across the dock to his berth. Quite how he imagined the tug could achieve that, himself being trapped flat alongside, was a mystery both to the tug Skipper and to me. After over an hour and missing two trains from the dock station while this flotilla leader was performing, I then asked if I could berth the ship for him so I could get home, at which point he agreed and simply disappeared off the bridge to leave me to it. There was a noticeable sigh of relief when he did vanish, and the ship was berthed in about ten minutes and I left to dash home ready for the next job to be issued.

Thankfully, not all Navy ships were like that and there were occasional light-hearted incidents which bucked the rules. One incident was when I took a Dutch corvette flying the NATO flag out from King George Dock in Hull, and on clearing the lock into the river, a sailor appeared on the open bridge (she was a rather ancient corvette!) wearing wooden clogs, one painted red and the other one green. I noticed that he had the red one on his right foot, and the green one on his left foot. Now everyone knows that red is for PORT (left) and green is for STARBOARD (right), so when I raised this with a twinkle in my eye, the Captain politely informed me that this was the STERN LOOKOUT, and this sailor immediately proceeded to the after end of the bridge and commenced lookout duties, staring astern. This of course placed his RED covered foot on the PORT side, and his GREEN covered foot on the STARBOARD side.

The other incident that 'bucked the system' was one winter's night when I was boarded on another minesweeper at the Spurn Light Vessel at 0300 on a very dark morning. I was met at the top of the pilot ladder by a smartly turned-out Petty Officer, who escorted me to the bridge, where I found the Captain in his bridge chair with his feet up on the window sill of the wheelhouse windows. Now this was unusual to say the least, and he was alone apart from the officer of the watch. He turned, still in his chair, and proffered his hand in a welcoming handshake. We exchanged a few details of the passage up the river to the dock, and he then merely said, "Well there you are Pilot, just ask for anything you need over the wheelhouse microphone, the lads down in the steering compartment below will comply, you can have any speed you want up to 16 knots, and if you don't mind I'm off down for a shower and shave before we get there." Still slightly mystified, I simply got on with taking the ship up to Albert Dock in Hull, arriving off the dock at the best time to make an approach and then fully expecting to hand over to the Captain for him to berth his ship, naval fashion. However, on arrival off the dock, I asked the Captain, who had appeared shaved and showered and dressed in warm clothing, whether he was going to dock and berth the ship, or whether he wanted me to do it? He immediately replied, "Please, carry on Pilot, you know what you're doing and I have little or no idea of the local conditions or practices so I'll be pleased to watch you do the job."

Albert Dock, Hull, showing the 'Bull Nose', the lock, and the river.

Slightly mystified but relieved that this job would hopefully go relatively smoothly and quickly, I turned the ship round through the 180 degrees to 'stem the tide' before dropping alongside the approach jetty and putting the ship into the lock, and then onto its berth at the oil bunkering station. It was only then that the mystery became clear. As he took off his heavy warm overcoat and thanked me for a faultless berthing, he asked whether I would like a dram to warm me up now that I had finished work. I saw that the insignia and stripes on his jacket indicated that he was from the Royal Naval Reserve, the 'Wavy Navy' as it had become known. The stripes on the cuffs of their uniform jackets were wavy rather than the more usual straight stripes which adorned the jacket sleeves of officers of the regular full-time Navy. I had been expecting the hordes of bodies to appear in the wheelhouse during the manoeuvre, but they didn't, and when the Captain realised that I was working it all out, I told him of my relief when that hadn't happened. "Oh no," was his reply, "we don't go in for all that bullshit here, at least when we haven't got a regular Navy officer on board with us, we're all from Manchester Liners here doing our annual two-week Royal Navy Reserve training, and we try to make it as professional as we can."

We repaired to the ward room and I spent a pleasant half hour chatting and sampling the contents of their whisky bottle before walking back to the Pilot Office. It only ever happened to me once, but it was such a refreshing change from what was, to us, the mayhem that prevailed on the bridge of a Royal Navy ship.

The Biggest Toasting Fork in the World

We had many differing types of vessel that entered the River Humber, from 300-ton coasters to 300,000-ton supertankers, and just about any sort of vessel in between those extremes of size that needed to reach places within the district. Many were straightforward, others difficult, but all in their own way interesting.

The Sail Training Association, a fine charity that provided opportunities for young people to sail away on a three-masted schooner for trips around the North Sea and sometimes beyond, owned two fine sailing vessels in the 1970s and '80s. These were the *Sir Winston Churchill* and the *Malcolm Miller*, and were officially exempt from the need to take a Pilot on the river as they were under the minimum prescribed compulsory length limit. As a body of professional men, we decided amongst us that for safety reasons and for the safety of all on board that we would waive any pilotage charges that would be incurred by these ships, and the authority also waived any boarding and landing fees charged for putting a Pilot on and taking them off when the ships came to the river.

When one of these two fine vessels arrived, there was always a bit of competition amongst us all to actually take these ships wherever they wanted to go. The rules, however, were always followed, and on one bright sunny morning, the *Sir Winston Churchill* arrived at the Spurn Light Vessel and was boarded by Tom Watson – a senior Pilot who relished the chance to pilot this lovely, graceful example of British design and build. In fact, the *Winston Churchill* was built at Dunston's Shipyard at Hessle on the River Humber, just five miles upstream from the Port of Hull, and designed by

Camper and Nicholson's of Southampton, a designer of many fine yachts and small ships, and it was followed a short while after by the *Malcolm Miller,* built and designed again by Dunston's and Camper's.

On this bright morning, Tom Watson suggested that as the wind was fair, the sails on the *Winston Churchill* could be raised, and he was happy to take the ship up to Albert Dock under sail. However, this request was considered by the Captain of the ship, and he said he preferred to proceed upriver on the engines alone. So, under power she proceeded up to Albert Dock in Hull.

The approach to Albert Dock in Hull was a little tricky, and many a brave Pilot had been deceived into attempting to go straight into the lock, which invitingly presents itself to the approaching ship with open arms, pointing down river as it still does to this day. However, with a strong tide behind, this approach is doomed to failure, and the intricate method of swinging the ship in the tideway off the dock, and then warping the ship into the lock around the 'bullnose' is the correct and only way to successfully achieve this manoeuvre. This sounds complicated but is in fact the sensible and seamanlike way of 'doing the job'. By swinging the ship around through 180 degrees in the river and putting it 'head to the tide', the Pilot immediately regains control of the ship in the immensely strong current flowing up the river and creates much more control over the movement over the ground. When a ship has the current behind her, she is in effect skating up over the ground at what can be an alarming speed, and it leads to all sorts of problems – not being able to stop before hitting the inner lock gates is one of them! After all, aeroplane Pilots don't land aircraft with the wind behind them for similar reasons! So, Tom swung the ship around and landed on the approach jetty to the lock, completely under control.

Now for the tricky bit. In order to enter the lock, the ship has to be turned back around the 180 degrees again to go bows first into the lock, and this is achieved by putting a rope out from the bows, but leading backwards to a bollard on the jetty to assist the swing and enter the lock in a controlled fashion. This does place a big strain on that particular rope, but it is done all the time and ships are built with strong points and provided with strong enough ropes to cope with this. So, Tom asked for this 'backspring' (as this rope is termed) to be put out and placed on the bollard on the quay. So far so good. The manoeuvre was then resumed with the ship's engines being put 'ahead' and the rudders angled to create the swing and to work against this restraining rope. The ship therefore started to go around the 180-degree turn to enter the lock.

Now while all this was going on, a Sunblest baker's delivery wagon appeared on the other side of the lock having been delivering to one of the ship's chandlers which were based on the dock estate. Seeing this magnificent sailing ship entering the lock under control and making a wonderful sight on that lovely morning, the driver parked his van on the opposite side of the lock, got out of his cab, rolled himself a cigarette and stood watching as the *Winston Churchill* edged slowly around the bullnose. Unfortunately, the backspring, under enormous strain, decided that it couldn't take any more and snapped, allowing the *Winston Churchill* to leap across the lock slightly out of control.

Before Tom could take action and stop the forward movement of the ship, the bowsprit of the ship – that graceful and elegant spar which overhangs the bow by some 20 feet and which was about 6 feet above the lock wall – pierced the side of this baker's van and went into the rear portion of the van by about 5-6 feet. The van driver stood motionless and in increasing incredulity as Tom, having regained control of the situation, backed the ship out again and resumed the manoeuvre with a fresh rope which had been hastily put out again by the *Churchill*'s crew. On backing out, the bowsprit brought with it a mix of bread cakes, loaves, baps, rolls and cakes, all freshly produced and destined for other consumers, and simply dumped them on the lock side and some even into the lock itself.

Afterwards in the office we sat and laughed at Tom's description of the incident, although he was somewhat reluctant to talk about it too much, such was his slight embarrassment. But I don't think there was one of us who wouldn't have loved to have been a fly on the wall in the bakery Transport Manager's Office later on that day when the driver of the van tried to explain how the damage had occurred, the loss of his precious cargo, and how he had been hit by 'The Biggest Toasting Fork in the World'.

Sail Training Association vessel, the *Sir Winston Churchill.*

Anyone for Tiffin?

Working and travelling on ships has many drawbacks and also many benefits, depending on what sort of ship you are on. Working for Alfred Holt and Company's fleet of fine ships, more often than not we enjoyed fine cuisine with lavish meals provided from the galleys and good service from our catering staff and stewards. My wife remembers one occasion when, on picking me up from London after a three-month voyage on the *Flintshire*, the Chief Steward playfully said to her, "I'd rather feed your husband for a week than a fortnight!" It was true that I have always enjoyed my food as my figure's profile will confirm, but the food on that particular ship was excellent with a good, balanced diet available and plenty of choice.

But adventures ashore held some surprises and some memorable meals at the various restaurants and establishments we visited, together with a lot of laughs. I suppose it all started when I took my then girlfriend (now my wife) to a very posh fish restaurant in Liverpool. I had just passed my 2nd Mates Certificate in Hull and, on travelling back to Liverpool where my wife was then at college, I decided to treat her to a fine lunch out. Entering the establishment, we were ushered to a table in the window by a very posh-sounding waiter who, after taking our drinks order, offered us the menu. He then went on to recommend the plaice, "Fresh in this morning sir, and coupled with the chef's finest French fries and fresh garden peas, it makes an admirable repast." Deciding that his recommendation sounded fine, we placed the order and sat back to await the arrival of the food. However, our suave waiter, on entering the kitchen through a double swinging door which rebounded open again, placed the order with the chef by yelling out in his more natural broad Scouse accent, "Fish, chips and peas twice there laa!" Gone was the sophisticated image, but the meal when it arrived was exceptionally nice!

Our travels around the Far East offered us many more opportunities to sample the cuisine that was there to be had, should you wish to try it. There were some of the officers and crew who wouldn't try anything 'foreign' and that was a shame because they didn't know what they were missing. One prime example was the Singapore Beach Road Satay Club, a rather primitive looking but perfectly sound way of sampling the delights of Malayan satay in all its glory. When my wife accompanied me on her voyage of discovery, we went to the Satay Club, which was situated within one of the many waterside promenade areas built by the British when they were in residence and in charge in Singapore. These green spaces were planted with grass and trees and interlaced with footpaths and small roads which at night were invaded by these small, wheeled, barrow-like stalls run by the vendors of the differing types of satay. These satay sticks were cooked over open fires contained within these 'barrows' and stools to sit on were provided for the diners around the stands and under the eaves of their overhanging roofs, should it happen to rain, which in Singapore it could and did with tropical ferocity!

Differing nationalities of ethnicity manned these stands, Singapore being a truly mixed race and multi-cultural place. If you wanted pork satay you had to go to a non-Malay vendor such as an Indian or Chinese barrow, but if you needed beef then you couldn't get that at a stand run by an Indian. If you wanted anything, you chose a Chinese vendor as they didn't have any religious hang-ups whatsoever! The pork, lamb, chicken and beef satay sticks were dished out for as long as you wanted them, and once you had had your fill, the bill was settled by simply counting the number of empty little wooden skewers on which your meat had been cooked that you had left in front of you! Drinks were provided by the little street urchins that hovered around the stalls, you simply gave them a couple of dollars and they would run to the nearest bar and return with cold beers to sate your thirst while you ate.

The markets on and around Bugis Street in Singapore also offered Chinese food to satisfy anyone's tastes, and when on the *Ajax* with Chief Officer Alan Shoesmith, who had previously spent quite a lot of time on the Singapore to Australia run on another of the company's ships, he had found all sorts of favourite street cafes where he would go and eat his fill. He took me to Bugis Street one night and I ate royally, tasting all sorts of different styles of Chinese food, which must be ranked alongside other cuisines as one of the most diverse.

Hong Kong provided very British-style food as well as the local Chinese cuisine, and one of my favourite haunts happened to be very close to the company's wharf in Kowloon. Blue Funnel owned their own exclusive wharf at which their ships would berth for the discharge of their outward-bound cargoes, and when homeward-bound loading on the buoys mid harbour, the launches that served to take us ashore used to land us at the wharf for convenience's sake. Close by was 'Mary's Bar', a veritable haven of peace without the inconvenience of the over-attentive bar girls that plagued us at other bars when ashore, offering you a 'good time' if you bought them a drink at overinflated prices! Mary's offered good wholesome food both of the European type and the local style if you so wished, and it was there that I developed my love of steak, egg and chips. To this day when asked by my wife what I would like to eat on any special occasion, I still trot out, "Steak, Egg and Chips," and even more occasionally, I get it!

But beyond Hong Kong on the schedule of port visits followed by the Glen Line ships that were part of the Alfred Holt and Company fleet, lies the 'Land of the Rising Sun' – Japan. Ashore, beyond the immediate port area and the sometimes seedy bars and bath houses that lure seamen into their clutches, there lies a food culture that is simple but incredibly satisfying and varied. Often, for a change, we would venture beyond those bars and bath houses to sample the varying ways that the Japanese prepare and eat their food. We were taken to a 'Yakitori' house by the local Port Chaplain of the Missions to Seamen for a noteworthy and very entertaining meal. This Chaplain was a very 'go-ahead' young minister who was determined to show seamen who visited that there was more to life in Yokohama than the first bar to stumble into when going ashore.

I repeated this trip when I had my wife with me and, although being unable to master the Japanese language in the short time he had been resident there, the Chaplain nevertheless managed to communicate with the waitresses what we would like to eat, much to their amusement as his methods were somewhat unconventional. For example, to order 'momo', which are chicken thighs, he would slap his own thighs; for 'tsukune', which are chicken meat balls he would point to his groin; for 'tebasaki' (chicken wings) he would flap his arms wildly; and for 'reba' (chicken livers) he would gesticulate towards his midriff at his side above his waist. But his forte was for 'sesame', chicken breasts grilled to perfection on skewers with a side salad of spring onions and salad vegetables, the actions of which should be obvious indicating well-endowed ladies with enlarged chests. This had the little Japanese waitresses in fits of laughter and laughing all the way back to the order hatch in the restaurant.

As in most places in Japan, in Kobe there were many small streets for shopping known as a 'motomachi', a cultural and retail shopping street that also offered eating houses. It was here I first sampled okonomiyaki, a style of cooking that is typically Japanese in that it is cooked right in front of you on a hot plate or 'teppan' and, once cooked, simply slid across the bar-style café seating to you with spatulas. Basically, it is a Japanese-style savoury pancake originally from Osaka, made from flour and eggs and filled with cabbage and the protein of your choice. It can be filled with anything, be it meat, fish or vegetables, and to sit there taking in the aromas and watch it being 'built' in front of you without fuss is heavenly.

But the crème de la crème of Japanese food also awaits in Kobe, where the famous Kobe beef steak is served from wood-fired barbecues that are pure ritual. The Tajima strain of black cattle that provide the meat are pampered to within an inch of their lives before being slaughtered to provide this delicacy. It is rumoured that they receive daily massages and are fed with beer to enhance the flavour of the meat and, if so, it comes through in every mouthful of the delicacy. The meat is heavily 'marbled' with fat and when grilled over a traditional wood-fired barbecue it virtually cooks itself. I for one will never forget eating at a beef steak house in Kobe one evening with my wife, Dai Jones the Chief Officer of the *Flintshire* and our host – the ship's agent in Kobe – a rather expensive meal ashore, but one not to be missed and one which will never be forgotten!

No trip to the Far East on a mainline Glen Line ship would have been complete without sampling one of 'Tiger's' curries in Penang. 'Tiger', a very large and statuesque Indian was the stevedore in charge of the gangs that came aboard when we anchored off Penang to load our last drops of cargo and fill the ship up before proceeding back to London to complete the voyage. It was one of the little perks that he loved to provide for the ship's officers while we were there, and to refuse would have been an insult to his Indian generosity, so every trip we dined in the Chief Officer's Office on a mix of Indian cuisine that was superb. Tiger would order the curry from the shore during the morning to be brought off by launch to the ship, and we would all gather to consume the delights at lunchtime when the stevedores had their lunch break, so no disruption to the cargo operations ensued. Aromas from the spices that were in those curries remained in the accommodation for a day or so after we had left Penang to sail across the Indian Ocean, a reminder of our stay in exotic lands that we would return to a couple of months or so later.

I had regaled Christine with stories and positive vibes about Tiger's curries, but unfortunately when, prior to our arrival in Penang, I was asked to swap ships and relieve the injured Second Officer on the *Glenfinlas*, which was outward bound from the UK, it was necessary to transfer from one ship to the other. So, Christine would have to forego that delight and miss out on her special curry. The two ships' schedules didn't marry up perfectly, but the solution was that Christine and I would leave the *Flintshire* in Penang, travel overnight by train from Penang to Kuala Lumpur, and then be taken to Port Swettenham to join the *Glenfinlas*, which was discharging in there at the time.

Looking forward to another trip around the ports of the Far East was uppermost in Christine's mind, and the prospect of more adventures were very exciting.

But one other meal stands out above most of the rest that I enjoyed in the Far East. In Communist Shanghai in the 1960s, we were not permitted to wander around on shore as we were in other countries on the scheduled trip around the Mystic East. When I took my wife with me on the *Flintshire*, I was fortunate enough to be sailing with a good bunch of fellow officers, who took it upon themselves to ensure that I could visit ashore with Christine, and if I was on duty they would also ensure that she was looked after if she wanted to go ashore to do some shopping. In Shanghai this meant accompanying her to the Friendship Store, the only place for shopping available in those dark days of Chairman and Madame Mao's strict regime. The Third Officer aboard *Flintshire* was an old friend, Peter Fraser. We had signed indentures on the same day in 1961, and I had only overtaken him in the promotion ladder as he had tried a spell ashore after obtaining his 2nd Mates Certificate, but had then returned to sea after he had proved to himself that shore life was not for him. On the morning of this unforgettable meal ashore, I was on duty supervising the loading of the cargo, and Peter offered to take Christine to the store to do some shopping, and then we arranged to meet in the Seamen's Club for lunch after I had been relieved at 1200.

In the ports around the world, there were clubs and missions that catered specifically for the visiting seamen who brought vital supplies to their countries, and took away their exports to bolster their national income. The Missions to Seamen, a Church of England organisation, did sterling work around the world, as did the Apostleship of the Sea, the

Catholic church's equivalent. However, in some places there were no religious institutions present, and indeed this was the case in Communist China, so here they provided what they loosely termed a 'Seamen's Club', just behind the famous bund in the heart of the port of Shanghai.

With typical Chinese inscrutability and ironic humour, the club was actually situated in the former, magnificent British Embassy building that had been lavishly built in Colonialist days. Placed in extensive grounds by the British to house their very important mission in that part of China, it was a grand example of opulence, resplendent with marble floors and huge marble columns surrounding a magnificent entry hall and reception area that had been used for diplomatic 'occasions' in the old days. This hall had around it a gallery at first floor level from which an impressive staircase wound its way down to the ground floor, and down which the Ambassador would descend to greet his guests.

However, when the British were expelled in no uncertain terms from China after the People's Liberation Army arrived in Shanghai, they had stripped the building of all its beautiful furniture and whatever fittings they could take with them, leaving behind a bare shell. When the Chinese then reopened the building as a club for visiting seamen, they had installed metal folding chairs and tin dining tables which were covered in plastic 'gingham style' checked pink and white tablecloths, creating an atmosphere that was totally at odds and inharmonious with the actual materials of the building itself. It created a weird and uncomfortable atmosphere, and to cap it all there were the usual heavily-armed guards patrolling in the gallery above the floor below, keeping a watchful eye on these 'bourgeois' decadent western seamen below them. Slightly intimidating and a bit scary as well, they were armed with machine guns that we assumed were loaded and ready for use should anyone step out of line.

So it was into this atmosphere that I arrived by taxi, travelling through the now rather neglected gardens of the vast estate where the embassy was situated, and entering the Seamen's Club to meet up with Peter and Christine who had already arrived. Peter had thoughtfully ordered some drinks – three bottles of Chinese beer that was the only beer brewed outside the United Kingdom in the proper fashion – no chemicals were used in the process and it tasted wonderful, particularly after a hard morning's work clambering up and down the hatch ladders on the ship. Each of these bottles was brought to the table already opened and contained two pints of this glorious amber liquid. I waded into mine with great relish while inspecting the menu of food on offer in the club. While we were contemplating what to order, our Boatswain and the No 1 Greaser from the ship entered with their families in tow. Chinese crews on the Glen Line ships were engaged via our own manning office in Hong Kong, but the people they recruited were all resident in Communist China, the bulk being from Shanghai. This meant for their families, a golden opportunity to catch up with their sailor husbands and fathers, albeit for a brief but valuable time together, and we on the ship made sure that any duties aboard were kept to a minimum to allow them this time for these family gatherings.

Greeting us from their own table, they saw we were about to order food, and kindly sent us another round of three more bottles of beer. Now my wife didn't drink great volumes of anything, and still doesn't, but we couldn't refuse and thanked them for their gift. When the waitress returned to take our order for food, we decided to sample the delights of the genuine Chinese cuisine on offer and opted for a bowl of chicken noodle soup each to start, to be followed by three different dishes: spicy beef, crispy fried pork and sweet and sour yellow fish, accompanied by a bowl of rice to complete the meal. I was particularly thirsty and had consumed the first bottle of beer and was part way down the second when I said to Peter that we should return the compliment and send a round of beers across to our Chinese shipmates on the nearby table. Christine was pacing herself with the drink, and then the soup arrived. Contained within a bowl the size of a small tureen were noodles piled as high as they could have been without toppling over the edge of the dish! It seemed like a veritable meal in itself, but we had ordered it so waded in and consumed most of the amazingly tasty soup that was hiding under the noodles in the bottom of the bowl.

Towards the end of the soup course, the second courses began to arrive. Platters the size of what seemed to be roasting dishes were placed in front of us, piled high and heavily weighed down with the spicy beef and the crispy fried pork. At the same time, the beers that we had sent across to our shipmates were returned and placed on the table beside us. The Boatswain came across and indicated that they were very grateful for the gift of the beers that we had sent, and hoped that we would enjoy our meal. It was realised afterwards that the guards above had noticed what had happened and if our crewmates had consumed those drinks that we had sent them, a non-complimentary report would have been lodged about them, which could have affected their families and friends, so they had to return them. We were then left with six pints of beer each to consume as well as all this huge, magnificent feast now placed before us on the table.

I'm afraid to say that when my wife gets a fit of the giggles, she is left helpless and can, without a shadow of exaggeration, be left almost completely breathless. She really has difficulty breathing, and her laughter is infectious, those around her cannot help but be drawn into these paroxysms of mirth. What set it off was the arrival of the sweet and sour yellow fish. They came on a platter that was about 60 centimetres long and 40 centimetres wide, and had reposed on it not one, but two enormous yellow fish, which were overhanging the ends of this platter. Christine started to laugh and even Peter was amazed at the tears streaming down her face while she shook uncontrollably from the sheer bizarreness of the situation.

Here we were in a Seamen's Club in Communist China, thousands of miles away from home, enjoying this sumptuous meal that was being brought to our table, and there was absolutely no way that we could possibly consume this huge amount of food placed before us, nor drink the six pints of beer each that we had ended up with. To cap it all, there were these inscrutable Chinese armed guards peering down from the gallery above at not only us, but other sailors at adjacent tables who had been drawn inexorably into the mirth being generated by Christine and the situation we had landed ourselves in. What was going through the guards' minds I cannot imagine; only that they could never begin to understand why these decadent western capitalists were behaving in such a fashion. To cap it all, it was not until we were in the taxi returning to the ship that I realised that the bowl of rice we had ordered never actually appeared!

A Bit of a Cock-up on the Catering Front?

On the long hauls up and down the length of the rivers along which we piloted ships, we were often royally entertained by the ships' officers and crews, and we spent many happy hours chatting with them. Tea was always offered to us, even in the vast number of continental ships that we handled, as it was assumed that, being British, that was our natural beverage! My personal preference was for coffee – tea made me want to visit the loo far too often – and so was no problem on the majority of ships that I piloted. There were, however, what we knew as the 'Cuppa Tea Boats', the ships that were British registered and manned by the steadfast and resilient 'Men of Kent'.

These ships were owned and managed mainly by two companies, the London and Rochester Trading Company, or the 'Crescent Boats' as we knew them, and another company based on the Medway, Messrs Lapthorns of Rochester. These ships and the way they were run was somewhat alien to us 'deep sea' men in that the crews were paid on a share basis – the more cargoes they carried the more money they earned – and it was very successfully based on the original raison d'être of the companies as barge owners. The crews fed themselves without any involvement from their owners, and I had many a good meal aboard one of the Crescent ships, generously offered to me by their crews. One of their hallmarks was that whenever you boarded them, their first enquiry in a broad Kent accent was inevitably, "Wanna cup o' tea Pilot?"

Coffee was more often offered on the multitude of

continental ships that we piloted, and it was usually always on the go on the bridges of the Scandinavian and continental ships that we boarded, and good coffee it was too! The way it was delivered differed in many ways, and on one occasion after I had boarded a very small Danish coaster the Master and his Chief Officer were in the wheelhouse waiting to greet me. After the initial pleasantries and sorting out what we were doing and where we were going, I settled down to con the ship up the river. The Master then said to me, "Oh by the way Pilot, the coffee is coming," only to be repeated by his Chief Officer with an enormous smile on his face who also said, "Oh ya, the coffee is coming!" Slightly mystified by the obvious amusement of the two of them, I waited for the joke to be shared. The ship, being only quite small, had an almost vertical staircase from the deck below to the wheelhouse with a door that opened into, rather than away from, the inside of the wheelhouse. After a short interval, the sound of heavy, almost elephantine footsteps was heard to be ascending these stairs, getting much louder as they approached. The door from stairway to wheelhouse was literally flung back, crashing into the bulkhead, and a rather large female cook marched across the wheelhouse, slammed a Thermos flask down on the small table at the front of the wheelhouse causing it to shake, and announced in a very deep voice, "COFFEE!" The only thing this young lady cook lacked was a Viking breastplate, a horned helmet and a sword, and after she had departed back down to her galley below in a similarly noisy fashion, the Master said, "That was the cook!"

Sadly, there were some occasions when the customary hospitality was not quite so forthcoming. I boarded a small Dutch ship at one of the topmost berths on the River Trent early one evening. It was crewed by a Master and wife team, the wife being the cook, and the rest of the crew were of mixed nationality, dubbed what we used to term a 'United Nations Crew' – cheap and not very efficient. The Master was keen to get going, but I advised him that we would have to wait for a while for the tide to rise as there wasn't enough water in the river to actually make the passage.

After about 20 minutes, the depth of water in the channel was sufficient, and with the rapidly rising tide we started to leave the berth and make a move. The Master then commenced to ignore me completely, issuing his own orders to his crew who let go of the ropes and we left the berth. He had an electric rudder control switch in his hands on a long wire lead, and refused to let me steer the ship, again ignoring my advice to pull away from the berth and cross the river at that point to find the channel and the deeper water. He simply informed me that he knew the river better than me and I could just stand around and keep quiet. I implored him to cross to the opposite side of the river before we ran aground, and again he simply snubbed me, carrying on in his own way. We came across quite a few of these clever young Dutch and German Masters who owned their own ships, and they were rather silly and obstinate when it came to taking advice from Pilots. We had learned the best way of handling them was to simply let them get on with it until they inevitably came to grief – you couldn't argue with them and it was best not to try! So I walked right out of the way to the after end of the funnel behind the wheelhouse leaving him to it, and just simply waited.

After about five minutes battling the very strong incoming rush of the tide, the inevitable happened, and we ground to a halt firmly stuck on the bottom to seaward of the berth we had left. The Master then appeared and said we were aground, to which I simply replied, "Yes," and nothing more. He then started to plead with me to help him, and I'm afraid that, without losing my temper, I wasn't very pleasant with him. I merely asked, "Why should I, as you say you know the river better than I do?" There was of course no answer to that, and I then agreed to take over the conning of the ship provided he did exactly as I asked. This was agreed, so on returning to the wheelhouse and taking the rudder control from him, I then asked for the main engines, which were still turning full ahead, to be stopped. A look of amazement appeared on the Master's face, and he queried even this action. With the engines stopped, however, the ship merely stayed aground for a few minutes until lifted clear of the river bottom by the rapidly rising tide, and we then crossed to the correct side of the river and proceeded outward.

I had noticed coffee being consumed by the crew before we left the berth, having been brought up by the Master's wife, although I was not offered one. However, after leaving the berth, grounding and re-floating, I asked for a coffee. I was informed that the galley was now closed, and I was offered a cold coffee from the pot in the wheelhouse by this clever, still slightly smirking Dutchman! Faced with a further four hours of battling the inrushing tide, this was not acceptable, but I kept quiet at that moment as I was rather busy, and steered the ship down the River Trent. On approaching the apex at the confluence of the Rivers Ouse and Trent and before entering the Humber, I stated to the Captain that he had two choices – either I got a hot coffee or I would turn the ship around, proceed to and tie up to the waiting jetty at Blacktoft on the River Ouse, order a taxi and go to a café to obtain a coffee, return later, and then cancel the passage to sea as we wouldn't have enough time or water to reach the open sea. I further pointed out that if this had been a British ship in Dutch waters with a Dutch Pilot on board, that Pilot would have insisted on a hot meal being provided. I wasn't asking for anything like that and he was totally in the wrong to refuse basic sustenance. The galley was, on this occasion, re-opened and I got my hot coffee!

Fortunately, that sort of situation didn't happen very often and we were mainly treated with respect. On another occasion, when piloting a large deep-drafted French tanker inward from the Humber Light Vessel towards one of the many jetties at Immingham, a large and very beautiful typical French meal was provided on the bridge while we were on passage to the berth. Included on the tray was a large carafe of red wine which would, if I had consumed it at that time, have broken my golden rule regarding drink – I would get drunk with anyone once I had finished, but I would never consume alcohol before, or during a job! As we approached the berth, the Jetty Master called me to say that the ship on the berth had not finished and had encountered problems, so I would have to return the French ship to sea and re-anchor at the Humber Light Vessel anchorage. After turning her around, I went back to the wheelhouse, relishing the tasting of the wine only to find out that the steward who had brought me the beautiful meal had returned and taken away the dirty plates from the tray together with the untouched carafe of wine, leaving me to finish the several small nuggets of delicious cheese without the accompaniment of the wine!

Ships' crews were being reduced during the 1980s and '90s to the detriment of the life on board many ships, and the large ships were not exempt from this lowering of standards. I had finished berthing a large Finnish tanker at the oil terminal one evening, and together with my Assistant Pilot was offered a sociable beer by the Master before proceeding home. The ship in question was one of a class of fine but aging ships built during the 1960s, lacking nothing in the way of comforts in the accommodation. Going down to the Captain's day saloon, he busied himself about getting a couple of beers from the fridge in his cabin while we chatted and I looked around at the splendour of the fittings in the cabin, the plush hardwood panelling on the bulkheads, the thick carpet on the deck, and the fine crafted wooden furniture that we were now reposed in. My gaze rested on a small plastic button in a panel on the bulkhead beside where my colleague was sitting, and underneath it was the title 'Steward'. These summoning buttons to call a steward were common in ships of that period, and I asked the Captain if the button was still working. "Oh yes," said the Captain with a wry smile flickering across his lips, "it works and sounds down below, and if I press it the bell rings, but nothing happens, no one comes!" And they say the Finns, like the Germans, have no sense of humour!

But probably one of the most memorable drinks during my career as a Pilot was that when, on returning home on my motorbike from the office very early one rather chilly spring morning after a long job and having got thoroughly cold, I decided that before I got into bed I needed a hot drink. Pondering the options, I decided that I didn't fancy tea, coffee would probably keep me awake, so I hit upon the brainwave of a cup of Bovril, that tasty and warming beef extract hot drink that always seemed to hit the right spot. In my semi somnambulant state, I spooned the extract from the small jar into my large cup, poured boiling water from the kettle to complete the brew, adding salt and pepper to season the beef, and then, being half asleep, I added a splash of milk and two sugars to complete the concoction. It wasn't until I had got undressed and laid down in bed beside my wife that I took my first sip of the drink, and I can assure you that I cannot recommend it at all! Far from sending me to sleep, it brought me back to full consciousness, and I had to get out of bed again and try to wash the disgusting taste from my mouth!

Small Dutch coaster, typical of the older type that visited the Humber regularly.
Photo courtesy of the Swansea and Port Talbot Historical Society.

The 'Foaming Cleanser'

After passing my Second Mates Foreign Going Certificate in May 1965, a peculiar rule of the Ministry for Transport was that although I was qualified, I could not receive my certificate until I reached the tender age of 20 years old! I planned to return to the company with whom I had served my apprenticeship and had trained me extremely well, Alfred Holt and Company's Blue Funnel Line, and they were willing to accept me into their sea-going strength as Fourth Officer. However, I was not able to join one of their 'deep sea' ships trading to the Far East while I did not actually have that piece of paper in my hand proclaiming me to have qualified as a deck officer. So, I started back with the company as an uncertificated officer on their ships that needed staff to 'coast' them – that was to relieve the deep sea officers on their return to the UK, and take the ships around the 'coast' while they proceeded home for their much needed leave between trips to foreign parts. This 'coasting' would mean taking the ships from Liverpool, their first port of call in the UK, on to Glasgow, the Bristol Channel ports, east coast destinations such as the River Humber, ports in Ireland and sometimes to Rotterdam and Hamburg. They would then finally return to Birkenhead to complete their loading for the Far East where I would leave again, relieved by the returning deep sea officers.

My first 'deep sea' ship was the *Asphalion* where I served for one voyage with Captain Noel James on his first deep sea command to the Far East. I got on very well with him and I served with him much later in my career as Second Officer prior to my departure to pastures new. However, although he wanted me back for a second voyage with him, events precluded this as the *Asphalion* was transferred to our Dutch subsidiary the Nederland Stoomvaart Mij Oceaan N.V. and the officers were all replaced by our Dutch counterparts. I then commenced my happiest time in Blue Funnel as firstly 4th Officer and then 3rd Officer on the 'Foaming Cleanser' – the *Ajax*.

MV *Ajax* at speed in the Malacca Straits, entering Port Swettenham in Malaya.

The *Ajax* was a newer ship of the company's fleet, and although a pleasure to serve on with some more modern innovations compared to the earlier 'A'-class ships, she had a few somewhat disturbing peculiarities. The 'Dizzy D's' as they were known suffered from a rather unfortunate flaw in their design, in that they lacked basic stability and had to be loaded extremely carefully to ensure they stayed with their blue funnels sticking 'upwards' and not inverted! Often entering Aden on the way home to receive fuel oil, the Captain could be heard to say to the Pilot, "No more than 10 degrees of rudder please Pilot; we are a bit 'tender'!" However, they were fine ships and had some modern stability gauges on board to help us keep them upright.

Characters abounded on board, not only amongst their Liverpool crews, but among their officers as well. The Captain was a Northern Irishman called O'Hanlon, affectionately known as 'Chrome Dome' or 'Uncle Fester' owing to him being somewhat follicly challenged. His wife was a domineering South African lady who ruled the roost at home, as did many wives of the day being left at home to cope while their husbands were away for much of every year that went by. So, one would suppose that on joining the ship to sail away again, he would reassert himself and rule the ship in a similar way to that which his wife ruled his home! He insisted on having his hair cut every week by the ship's barber, one of the Chinese Engine Room Greasers, and whereas everyone else paid this crew member for his trouble, O'Hanlon considered it his right to not have to pay! He also had the annoying habit of addressing his officers as, "Mr. 'er 'er 'er." He knew our names full well but never used them, just pointed.

He and our Chief Engineer, Fred Stansfield, used to argue incessantly while eating their meals in the saloon, much to the annoyance of all others dining at the same time, it was just an upshot of that 'oil and water' syndrome where deck and engineering officers were supposed never to mix! One of their main arguing points was freemasonry. Fred, bless him, was a single man and was actually a freemason belonging to a lodge in Kingston upon Hull, his home town. But Captain O'Hanlon, being a Northern Irishman and a Protestant, belonged to an Orange Order chapter – something of a controversial subject in those dark times of the 1960s when Orangemen and Catholics were at loggerheads. It was rather wrongly perceived that the Orangemen became freemasons simply so that they could 'cock a snook' at their Catholic countrymen who were not allowed to keep secrets from their priests, whereas their Protestant counterparts were not bound by such strict rules. This discussion would be carried on after lunch by Fred, who would collar anyone prepared (or not!) to listen to him. We had plenty of warning of Fred's approach, however, as he had very bad feet – a result of being a prisoner of war in the 1940s – and he wore special shoes which squeaked as he walked, earning him the nickname of 'oink-oink'. This squeaking would be heard as he reached the deck that contained the officers' cabins and the cabin doors would shut in succession as he made his way down the alleyway hoping to catch some unsuspecting person with whom to have a good rant. He never came into your cabin, just stood in the doorway and rambled on forever, denying you that precious couple of hours of extra sleep during your off-watch period that you had foregone the night previously!

My first voyage on the *Ajax* I served as 4th Officer, being on the 4- to 8-watch with the Chief Officer, Bryan Hurst; known throughout the fleet as 'Railway Hurst'. Bryan was a nice bloke to work with, but his enthusiasm for building his own railways became a bit of a sore point with the rest of the officers as he was somewhat obsessed, and his railways could sometimes take precedence over his official shipboard duties. These duties were often taken on and covered by the other officers while he whiled away his time constructing railway tracks for his layout at home. It was rumoured that he had his house designed and built around a cellar to take his railway layout, and this was proved to me some time afterwards when, whilst visiting my wife's parents in Bristol, where Bryan also lived, we encountered him and gave him a lift in our car. He invited us back to his house and showed us his massive 'O' gauge railway layout in the basement level of his home, which was actually elevated to allow the railway to go out into his garden and around a loop before returning inside! The garden was festooned with bonsai trees – to scale of course! – to add atmosphere to this rather impressive layout. Bryan's only regret in life was that he and his wife produced two charming daughters, who sadly were not in the least bit interested in model railways!

The traditional ship's arrival telegram prior to going into Hong Kong on that first trip included a message for Bryan, informing him that his 5,000 sleepers were ready. On arrival at the berth, several metal biscuit tins were delivered containing these accurate scale versions of the traditional railway sleepers, manufactured in hardwood at a very cheap rate in Hong Kong, and all soaked in creosote to preserve them. Bryan was cock-a-hoop and immediately started to construct a complicated interchange system; I think it was something like a double diamond crossover with points and Lord knows what else! Unfortunately, my cabin was next to the ship's office, which Bryan had commandeered as his workshop, and the sound of a toffee hammer tap, tap, tapping away into the wee small hours every night at sea as he hammered the small pins to attach the rails to these sleepers would keep me awake. The following morning at 0400 I would be on watch with Bryan who had worked for most of the night on his railway, and he used to come on to the bridge, immediately lay down on the chartroom settee to catch up on his missed sleep, leaving a bleary eyed me to keep the watch in his absence. I have to actually hand it to Captain O'Hanlon as it was he who realised eventually what was going on and told Bryan to desist as it wasn't doing me any good.

The second trip on the *Ajax* was much more relaxed, as

Bryan had been promoted to Master in the company, and was replaced by Alan Shoesmith, a Scot from Tayside who was a totally different character and a pleasure to work alongside. He was a single man who had spent much of his career serving on the trade operated by the company between Australia and the ports in Malaya and the China Sea, the ships never returning home to the UK. He relished the opportunity to return to the 'main line' ships, and his appointment to one of the notorious Dizzy D's was a feather in his cap. We got on like a house on fire and worked well together while on watch. No more sleepless nights on that trip, which was short and curtailed by events within the company which determined that we picked up another one of the company's ship's homeward schedule, owing to that ship having been involved in an incident in China.

At the end of that second trip, Captain O'Hanlon asked me to return for another voyage, and promised me promotion to the dizzy heights of 3rd Officer. I of course readily accepted and came back again after a shortened leave to re-join. It was then that I met the redoubtable Dave Chambers who joined the ship as 2nd Officer. Dave and I became instant, firm friends and that relationship has carried on through thick and thin to this day. His wife Sally and my wife Christine also got together and came to 'meet us in' after that memorable trip together, and to our surprise and utter amazement it was Captain O'Hanlon who invited them to come on board when we arrived in the lock at Liverpool, and travel with us through the docks to our berth.

There was another event during that third voyage on the *Ajax* that deserves mention. The ship had got a little out of sync with the regular schedule timings she had to keep, due to us having to relieve another ship the trip previously. Schedule dates were advertised sometimes months in advance, so in order to catch up with our normal dates we were somewhat pushed around and had some time spent doing not a lot! One of those periods was when we arrived at Bangkok, and we spent the Christmas and New Year period anchored off the port for two full weeks, awaiting a berth and slotting back into our normal schedule. We had anchored on 22nd December and observed over the next couple of days a British Ben Line ship, the *Benmachdui*, anchoring also to await a berth. There was a Hong Kong registered ship, flying a red ensign, and a Swedish ship also close by in the anchorage.

On Christmas Day morning, Captain O'Hanlon, in an uncustomary mood of bonhomie, appeared on the bridge where I was keeping an anchor watch and instructed me to launch the motor lifeboat. As 3rd Officer I was officially 'in charge' of the motor lifeboat, a particularly powerfully engined boat with a much meatier 4-cylinder Thorneycroft water-cooled diesel, rather than the Petter air-cooled diesels fitted to most of the other ships' lifeboats in the fleet. The Captain asked me to go first to the *Benmachdui*, then the Hong Kong registered ship and the Swedish ship to invite the Master, Chief Engineer and Chief Officer of each ship to come to us for a pre-Christmas Day luncheon drink. Taken somewhat aback by this display of sociability which seemed totally out of character for our crusty 'Chrome Dome', I launched the boat and, accompanied by an engineer and a couple of the Midshipmen, we did the rounds. The *Benmachdui* readily accepted the invitation, but as the Master and Chief Officer couldn't leave the ship at the same time, it was just the Master, Chief Engineer and 2nd Officer who accepted. The same happened at the Swedish ship, but at the Hong Kong registered ship there was a total and rather curt dismissal of the invite, so we proceeded back to the *Ajax*, collecting the senior officers who had accepted. I resumed my watch on the bridge, and there followed a jolly little party in our ship's lounge. Being relieved at 1200 by the 4th Officer, I proceeded down to the saloon where I ate the traditional Blue Funnel Christmas Day light luncheon – the main Christmas meal followed much later in the day.

My good friend Dave Chambers inviting anyone to 'guess the name of the ship'.

Just a short while after I had finished my luncheon, I was asked by the Captain to take the Swedish and the other British officers back to their respective ships, and on coming alongside the Ben Line ship, the Master asked me to return to our ship and invite the Master, Chief Officer and anyone else who wanted to come, to return and have lunch with them aboard the *Benmachdui*. This I did and as I had already had my lunch, I didn't join the others in the *Benmachdui*'s saloon for the festivities. I was, however, provided with a case of cold beer, and I settled down on the boat deck in the shade, where I did fair justice to the case of beer! There were several kindly visits from the officers of the *Benmachdui* to check that I was OK, and we all gathered together after their lunch and continued for a while until the case of beer had vanished. There was then the task of conveying my senior officers back to the *Ajax* – our 2nd and 3rd Engineers, Chief Officer Alan Shoesmith and 2nd Officer Dave Chambers among them.

I'm afraid by this time I was somewhat worse for wear and, upon being asked to re-board the boat tied up alongside the *Benmachdui*'s gangway and navigate it back to the *Ajax*, I apparently replied, "Oh never mind the boat, we'll get a taxi back to the ship!"

My good friend Dave has never let me live that one down!

'Luftkissenfahrzeug'

"A what?" Yes, that's the German for a hovercraft, or an 'Air Cushion Vehicle' in literal terms.

During our time training and getting experience on the hovercraft that we flew, my colleagues and I who commenced our amphibious hovercraft training in the latter part of 1971 got to learn all sorts of new skills and facts about those wonderful machines. We had all spent a full season on the Hovermarine HM2 'air cushion vehicle' that was not amphibious; they could only operate on water as their propulsion was by conventional water propellors. These craft gave us experience of operating high-speed craft in congested waters, and carried out a service between Portsmouth Harbour Station and Ryde Pier on the Isle of Wight. While they were supported on a cushion of air which enabled them to travel at speeds of up to 40 knots, they could not land on a pad at a hovercraft terminal – that would not have done their water propellors much good! So, they operated between modified berths which could also be used by conventional boats.

The decision to 'stretch' the amphibious SR.N6 hovercraft that operated the Cowes to Southampton route was taken in that year, and was a forerunner to the later stretching of the huge SR.N4 Mountbatten craft that plied their trade on the English Channel between Dover and Boulogne/Calais. Thus, more flight crew were needed, and John Summers, Ken Blackwood and I, having spent our first season on the Portsmouth to Ryde route as temporary flight crew, were interviewed and accepted as permanent staff to train and then assume roles as Commanders on both routes. This entailed moving to the Isle of Wight to take up residence and to commence a period of intense training before being licensed.

During that time, we got to fly all sorts of different SR.N6 craft as the two SeaSpeed craft (*009* and *011*) were removed from service and taken to the manufacturer's factory in East Cowes to be 'stretched' – cut in half and an extra ten foot section grafted into the middle. Part of the deal that was struck between SeaSpeed and the British Hovercraft Corporation (BHC) was the charter and use of two of their standby stock (*016* and *028*) both for training and to run the daily service between Cowes and Southampton. These two craft were basically the same as all the others, but with differing interiors and equipment. They handled the same, but their older radios, intercommunication systems and navigational equipment could catch us out and cause us a few problems.

Part of the training consisted of 'systems' familiarisation, the engine set up and installation, and all the ancillary systems connected with the overall set up and running of the craft. The fuel delivery system was fairly straightforward until it came to the actual engine, but we did a one-week course at Rolls Royce to learn all about the latter before we were even allowed to sit in the seat and start the engine. One of the basic rules was that on completion of service for the day, the Low-Pressure Fuel Shut Off Valve – the 'LP Cock' – was shut off to prevent fuel dribbling at low pressure from the tanks onto the ground while the craft was parked overnight, should it develop a fuel system leak. This was a basic rule for any aircraft, which transmitted down to the hovercraft. In SeaSpeed this valve was never shut off between flights, only at the end of the day, but in Hovertravel (our sister company that ran from Ryde to Southsea) their Commanders were taught to shut the valve whenever they left the craft, even for a few minutes. This didn't bother us in SeaSpeed until one year we had one of their Commanders flying for us. We were short staffed after one of our own Commanders resigned at short notice, so SeaSpeed hired Tony Caulkwell in to cover. On one day after Tony had been flying in the morning, and I came to relieve him at 1330 to assume command for the remaining flights of the day, I started the engine prior to take off, and didn't notice anything odd until I cleared the breakwater and started to increase engine power to accelerate away towards Southampton.

Even opening the manual hand throttle to fully open, I couldn't get the engine to increase revs above 24,000rpm, whereas the normal maximum operating revs were 25,400rpm. I was about to call the base engineers to see if there was a problem when I suddenly remembered the LP Cock and, glancing down at my feet where this valve was positioned to one side of the platform, where we sat to drive the beast, I noticed that indeed this valve was firmly in the closed position. Feeling a little embarrassed and rather stupid, I eased the hand throttle down to reduce the demand on this valve, flicked it open with my right foot, and then accelerated away to continue the trip to Southampton.

Later, relating this story to another one of the small team of Commanders, I found out that I wasn't the first to suffer this embarrassment of following Tony Caulkwell in the seat, and others had also experienced this 'phenomenon'. It was rather an amazing fact that the engine could have even been started with this valve shut. I suppose it gave testament to the 'usefulness' and efficiency of the valve!

The radio systems in the differing craft also varied. Our two SeaSpeed craft were fitted with simple modern transistorised VHF radio sets which were compact, easy to operate and had an internal facility to provide a headset link between Commander and Navigator when this was required, for example at night or in fog. The complete unit of these sets was placed beside the Commander's seat and controlled from that position. The banter between driver and his 'seeing eyes' on the radar was via headsets and was formal and to the point when required. But on a clear night the exchanges between them were usually merely to confirm what the Commander who was driving could actually see through the windows, and whether he was on a course that would avoid collision with anything he may not be able to see, such as the 'blind' buoys and beacons that had no lights on them and were used as secondary channel markers. So, between these highly important conversations for the safety of the craft we could, and did, discuss all sorts of other things. Not requiring any water at all to travel over, we stayed out of the main shipping channels as much as we could to avoid close encounters of any kind, so we needed to know where these unlit objects were. Approaching the River Itchen at the end of the flight could also be a bit fraught – many unlit markers used by the Pilots of the large ships that used the Solent and Southampton Water were present and had to be avoided.

Both the BHC owned craft had somewhat archaic VHF radio systems installed, and *028* had an ancient, rather large, valve powered Redifon radio set which was actually situated under the rear seat at the back of the passenger compartment, with a remote control panel situated alongside where the Commander sat at the opposite end of the craft. On the front of this large and cumbersome radio set box at the back of the craft was a switch that activated the speaker on the radio set itself, and which was kept in the 'OFF' position so that the conversations over the intercom between

Commander and Navigator were kept strictly private, both of them wearing headsets to communicate with each other.

One night towards the end of a flight approaching the Itchen, I was navigating for Ken Blackwood who was flying the craft, and was informing him of all the unlit beacons and generally assisting him to avoid any mishaps on the approach. Eventually, when he had all these things visual and he was happy, he simply said to me over the headset, "Thanks Jeremy, I think I can manage to f*** it up from here."

On landing at the terminal and starting to disgorge our passengers, one of the regulars who had been sitting at the back of the craft thanked us for a smooth flight as he left the craft and added, "I see you managed to f*** it up OK then Ken." I'm afraid both our faces fell a mile, and we wondered what had been going on. I put my headset back on and Ken went to the back of the craft while I said a few words into my microphone. The words boomed out loud and clear through the cabin, emanating from the speaker on the radio set, and we realised that the whole of our conversations throughout that particular crossing had in fact been broadcast loud and clear to a large majority of our load of passengers. We had naturally assumed that our conversations had been just between the two of us, never thinking for a moment that anyone else could hear us. Someone had obviously unknowingly knocked this switch to the 'ON' position, probably with the heel of his shoe while settling down in his seat over this radio box, and opened up a line of communication that was definitely not intended!

Rather embarrassingly we realised we had also been discussing all sorts of subjects in between our necessary navigational chatter, and some of these subjects were a bit risqué, to say the least. Ken was not married and was 'playing the field' as it were, and wasn't backward at discussing some of the more intimate moments of his courting.

Afterwards, when we arrived back in Cowes, we ensured that this offending switch was taped into the 'OFF' position to avoid any further embarrassing incidents.

Even now, 50 years later, both Ken and I remember that dark night when we discussed the world in general, some of the young ladies' attributes that Ken had encountered, and more pointedly our acute embarrassment when we discovered that we had been 'found out'.

Redifon radio remote control box, top right-hand corner of photograph!

Hull Roads or Bust

At the start of each 'cruise' or 'sea station' as it was known in the early days of my career as a Humber Pilot, the oncoming crew for the day would assign six of its strength to travel to Spurn Head where the Pilot Station was situated, and they would be on standby around the clock for the next 24 hours to go off to board ships that arrived and needed a Pilot to take them to anchor inside in the more sheltered part of the river. They would also be available to take ships that arrived after high water to their destination, when normal boarding from the bulk of the Pilots on duty had ceased. The accommodation at Spurn Point was very comfortable, there being six bedrooms and a full catering facility with a steward on duty 24 hours a day. Life was sometimes very quiet on 'the base' as it was known, but at other times very busy with the occasional very unusual job thrown in for good measure.

Being a junior Pilot, I was very much the one who would get 'by-passed' when larger ships came in for the anchorage, or the odd ferry that would arrive after high water to proceed to Immingham, those ships being 'too big' for me to take. As a Third-Class Pilot I was restricted to 16 feet draft and 1,500 tons 'Nett' – another peculiarity of the day when measuring ships' sizes, and could often end up at the end of the 24 hour period having done nothing while my more senior colleagues may have done two or three jobs in the time on the base. But this sometimes worked to my advantage, and I could sometimes drop for the 'quick job' or the slightly 'out of the ordinary' job.

This was certainly the case in the early hours of one morning when the Pilot Master rang me to say that he was boarding me 'out of turn' as he had a rather unusual job for me

– particularly as sailing had been my hobby when I had lived and worked in Cowes on the Isle of Wight. The *Hydrogen*, a restored Thames spritsail barge was approaching the river from the south and required the services of a Pilot to take her to Hull Roads. She was in fact bound upriver to York – an unusual destination for us Lower Station Pilots, but nevertheless her Master wanted a Pilot and although not my turn in the rotation of availability, Reg Baldwin, the Pilot Master, decided that I was the man for the job. I had some garbled message from Reg that the ship wanted to go as far as Immingham and anchor there, and then proceed up to Hull Roads to be met by a steam tug from York that would be coming down to Hull on the next tide. This lovingly preserved steam tug from the early 1900s would then tow the *Hydrogen* up to York over the course of a couple of tides, where she would stay for a few weeks before coming down again to proceed onward on the next phase of her programme.

Going off on the launch to find and to board the *Hydrogen* was great fun. These old barges had a small engine that was not very powerful and provided what little electricity there was available for them. On that dark morning we had difficulty spotting her as her lights were extremely dim, being oil lamps from the old days, and the Launch Coxswain had to be guided towards her by Reg in the tower using the powerful radars that were installed in the control tower.

On boarding her I introduced myself to the Master, and we commenced our passage up the river. I started to clarify with the Master what his wishes were, and I asked why he wanted to anchor off Immingham. His reply was that he didn't think that they would make it as far as Hull Roads, that was too far on what was left of the incoming tide, it being by then two hours to high water with not much current left. I then enquired why we were under sail and not power, which would have helped, and he explained that on leaving his previous port of Lowestoft, they had been under power with some of the sails up as well. The wind had picked up from the east and heeled the barge over. Now, the 'retro fitted' engines in those old barges had been installed long after their original build, and had been installed for convenience on the starboard side of the main keel with associated cooling water suctions for the engine also on the same side. As the barge had heeled more and more with the effect of the strengthening wind pressing on to the sails, the water suction on the hull had come out of the water, and the engine, being starved of cooling water had seized solid, coming to an abrupt halt. They had contacted the owner who had told them to carry on to the Humber and the engine would be sorted out in York.

Quickly weighing up the situation, I asked and suggested that we 'hang the washing out' – in other words get lots more sail on her as she only had her mainsail and foresail up at the time. The wind was in the absolute right direction, following us up the river, the tidal stream was possibly just enough to carry us all the way to Hull Roads in one go, and I was quite happy to have a go at it! They called out the rest of the crew (all two of them) and they proceeded to put up the jib, the jib topsail, the topsail and the mizzen. And did she fly! I took the wheel to relieve the crew, and only being light drafted and it being towards high water, we started to cut the corners off to 'straight-line' the trip up the river, ironing out the bends and kinks in the channels which would have added great distance to the trip. The speeds we reached were quite phenomenal and the buoys and points of the passage slipped by with remarkable rapidity. We did at one point pass a very slow old coaster that was also making its way up to Hull Roads, slightly to the annoyance of the Pilot who was taking that ship up the river!

In conversation with the Master, I enquired as to why they were going to York. In reply, he simply took out the signalling lamp and shone it on the mainsail. There emblazoned in large white letters was the logo: Bells Scotch Whisky. All became clear as she was on charter to Bells as a promotional tool, and she attracted many buyers and vintners to the parties that were held on board. Down below was a sumptuous saloon where cargoes had once been carried, and she was a perfect organ to promote that product from Scotland alternatively referred to as The Staff of Life, Scottish Morning Dew and many other affectionate titles. I had been asked when I boarded if I wanted a hot drink, and as I was on the wheel on the open deck in early March, I had said, "Yes," hoping for whisky laced coffee to be forthcoming. My hopes of that were unfortunately dashed as it was explained that although they promoted the stuff, they didn't carry any on board!

As I had asked for the sails to be rigged as soon as they could, they hadn't called the stewardess straight away but had got on with 'hanging out the washing'. The coffee did eventually appear via the traditional companionway, a structure that was watertight in bad weather, and was so positioned so as not to allow any breeze to be carried down below and extinguish the galley fire or the oil lamps in the saloon below. This companionway concealed a ladder that allowed people to ascend to the deck, and vice versa, and as the light was streaming out from this hatchway, anyone who came up the ladder was in total shadow. Bearing in mind this was about 0300 in the morning when the coffee arrived, I was surprised to be greeted by the stewardess proclaiming, "Good Lord Jeremy, what are you doing here!" At first I could not see who was addressing me, but when she stepped out of the gloom and into the light that was behind her, I then recognised her as one of the SR.N4 hovercraft hostesses that had been working in Dover during my time with SeaSpeed on the English Channel. I had last seen Chloe in a hotel bar in Dover while we all had a drink together after completing the day's services across the Channel. We reminisced about the 'Good Old Fun Days' that we used to have in Dover, and how she had moved on to other things. She adored doing this job, which was different to say the least, and she just loved the camaraderie and the life aboard the barge.

She went on to ask what I had been doing since I left SeaSpeed, and we recalled other past friends and colleagues from those heady days flying across the Channel. It was Chloe, when I had asked for some advice on buying perfume for my wife in the Duty-Free shop at the terminal in Boulogne, who had willingly come with me to the shop and advised me to buy Chanel No. 19 instead of the rather more run of the mill and usually purchased Chanel No. 5. My wife has loved it ever since.

Later, as we approached Paull and Saltend Jetties, the tide and the current did die away completely, and it was only because the tide was a neap, a smaller tide than usual, that the outgoing current didn't take charge for another 20 minutes or so – just sufficient with the wind still fresh from the east behind us so that we actually did make it to the anchorage in the East Roads. Much relieved and grateful after we had anchored, the Master issued a very kind invitation for my wife and family to come to York and enjoy his hospitality while the barge was alongside at York. Sadly, this was not possible as I had just started my 'sea station', committed to a period of duty of two full weeks, and on my last working day of that period I passed the *Hydrogen* outward bound for

Leith, her next port of call. I exchanged pleasantries over the airwaves with the Master and Chloe, and I wished them 'Bon Voyage', advising him mischievously, and somewhat tongue in cheek, to ensure that the cooling water intakes remained below the water line!

It was the largest sailing craft that I had ever sailed, and she was indeed beautiful to handle. Her grace and the way she ploughed through the water was a delight, and to say I sailed her was probably a bit of an exaggeration, I had the benefit of an experienced Sailing Master to help me. But the courses I took and the corners I cut made the whole thing possible and saved the ship another tide's delay on her passage up the river.

To my knowledge the *Hydrogen* is still in service today, being available for charter for days out and weekends away. She now carries people instead of cargoes, but retains her grace, charm, intrigue and beauty. Photograph courtesy of Nick Ardley.

"Very Sorry, But Tonight Lady Take Off ALL Clothes!"

Wives on ships were very much a new thing in the 1960s and '70s, and while Masters and Chief Engineers on merchant ships were permitted to take their wives with them for the long deep sea voyages, lower ranks were also permitted to have their wives accompany them on the shorter coastal voyages while the ships were 'coasting' around the UK and European ports. However, in 1969, Alfred Holt and Company, with whom I was serving as a Deck Officer, decided to allow their more junior officers to also apply for permission to take their loved ones with them. At the time I was a Third Officer, but at the same time the company decided to have a re-shuffle of the ranks of their deck officers, and I was promoted to Second Officer, just at the same time as the permitted rank of allowing wives to accompany them was lowered to Second Officer!

I had served on Glen Line's cargo passenger liner the *Flintshire* as Third Officer for almost a year at that time, with the redoubtable Captain Raddings as Master, a perfect gentleman with whom I got on particularly well. He and I worked in conjunction with the weather forecasts and weather predictions that were vital to safe passage making in the sometimes treacherous waters of the South China Sea, and avoiding the regular horrendously vicious storms that invaded the area in the typhoon season was essential. These typhoons were of such a strength that they had to be avoided, and predicting their tracks in those early days was something of an 'educated guessing game' after receiving the latest bulletins from the weather forecasting authorities. There were no computer predictions such as there are in this modern day and age, and experience was everything. Gordon Raddings was very astute in this skill, and I learned a lot from him about that 'science' that was, in those days, vital to avoid a catastrophe.

With the new regulations regarding wives in mind, I went to him to ask for his permission to write to the company to request that my new wife of some nine months could accompany me on the next three-month deep sea voyage to the Far East, and permission from the company was subsequently given. The only fly in the ointment was that later in that voyage Captain Raddings himself also received a letter from the company to confirm that he was being promoted to one of the new 'Priam'- and 'Glenalmond'-class vessels currently under construction, and he was to become the new Master of the *Protesilaus* and take her on her maiden voyage. A real testament to his skills and reputation as a Master, and a feather in his cap. Sadly, it also meant that we would have a new Master on the *Flintshire* for the next voyage, and Gordon Raddings would not be there.

So, I set off with my wife, Christine, in tow, for a truly remarkable voyage to the Far East via the Cape of Good Hope; the Suez Canal still being closed after the Six Day War of 1967. I saw more on that voyage of what was supposed to be three months to the day than I did in my preceding eight years with the company – the nearest bar and restaurants having been our standard 'run ashore' to relax after the hard graft of working a cargo passenger liner in the 1960s. But with Christine accompanying me, I had to make the effort to visit some of the more notable tourist sights and sounds of the mystical Far East, and our schedule was, as always, on the Glen Line 'L'-service. We sailed from London, and in sequence visited Las Palmas for bunkers, direct to Singapore via the Cape (with a call at Cape Town for mail) then Hong Kong,

Manila, Shanghai, Yokohama, Shimizu, Nagoya, Kobe, back to Hong Kong again and then Singapore, Port Swettenham (now Port Klang) and Penang, before returning to London again via the Cape. Three months to the day, sailing on 24th August 1969 and returning to London on 24th November, you could set your watch and calendar by her schedule!

The days were made so much easier by having a good set of fellow officers, who bent over backwards to ensure that if I wanted to go ashore for a full day, they would cover for me and allow me to make up the hours I owed them at a time convenient to me. The new Master who joined the *Flintshire* for that trip was a little 'put out' that my wife was there, as he hadn't actually authorised it, not being there on the previous voyage when permission had been sought. However, he accepted the fact and we got on tolerably well after a few initial awkward 'interviews' where he laid down the law regarding Christine not generally mixing with the passengers. This led to her having an extremely relaxing break for most of that voyage, in contrast to her teaching duties at Purbrook Park County Grammar School where she was the Head of the Girls' Physical Education Department. A relief had been organised for her so that she could take leave of absence from her teaching duties, so all was set for her holiday!

There were many instances where we enjoyed the runs ashore, and even more little incidents on board where we got so much pleasure and amusement, such as the incident of the 'Where, Where Bird'.

One of my many duties on board was that of Meteorological Officer, a role that I enjoyed and shared with all the other officers. The *Flintshire*, being on a regular scheduled run was identified by the Meteorological Office in the UK as a 'weather ship', and our duties were to observe the weather conditions every six hours and transmit the results to the various radio stations that we were close to on our journeys across the oceans. These observations which were vital to the Met Offices of all nations around the world for weather forecasting were recorded in a 'rough copy' on the bridge, and it was my duty to copy them into a fair copy before arrival back in the UK, where an official from the Met Office would meet the ship in when she docked in London, and take the books away. At the back of this book were several blank pages where we could append any strange or unusual meteorological observations or happenings while we kept watch on the bridge. Any such sightings or happenings would enhance the ship's reputation for this work and resulted in me being given a couple of 'prizes': one a Philips *World Atlas* and the other a Collins *English Dictionary*, both of which I still have to this day.

It was up to all my fellow officers to make entries on to these 'extra pages' and when I arrived on the bridge to relieve Peter Fraser, the Third Officer on the 8-12 watch, he told me of an observation he had made during his previous watch, which he had entitled 'The Where-Where Bird'. Mystified, I read on and could not help showing it to my wife. She had expressed a keen desire to see whales, which we usually encountered in various places during the passage out to the Far East. Our cabin was immediately below the starboard wing of the bridge, and the arrangement with all the other officers was that if a whale was sighted, they would dash out on to the starboard bridge wing and stamp loudly on the deck immediately above our cabin so that Christine could run out of the accommodation to see the whale. Peter thus appended the observation pages with the story of the 'Where, Where Bird', explaining that if the officer of the watch stamped on the deck on the starboard bridge wing, a bird would dash out of the accommodation shouting, "Where? Where?" and looking eagerly over the side and into the distance searching for the elusive whale! That observation did not go into the final fair copy book for submission!

Our outward journey was subject to many happy trips ashore, and I saw many sights that I had never seen before. Interlaced with all this were the things that we bought for our new home back in England, and the shopping expeditions were memorable. Money was tight, but we made the most of it and were dutifully rewarded with many trinkets and household items that we still own today. In Shanghai in Mao Tse-tung's time as supreme ruler in a very red Communist China, we were restricted as to where we could go, and when we went ashore we had to travel by taxi – we were not allowed to walk about the town at all. Everywhere was a sea of drab colours, dark greys and greens with the only relief being splashes of brilliant almost crimson reds to accentuate the red nature of the culture. Shopping was restricted to the Friendship Store, and if we wished to visit we would request of the armed guard at the top of the gangway for a taxi to be summoned. On arrival we would board the taxi at the foot of the gangway to be taken direct to the door of the store.

On the first occasion I took my wife to the store to do some shopping, we arrived and she was sitting on the near side of the taxi adjacent to the kerb. Shanghai at the time was a place of transition; people from all over China would throng there to seek work, and the place was a sea of heaving humanity waiting to be allocated jobs, both in that city and in the immediate surrounding areas. Most of these people had never seen a European woman before, such was the repressive control over the population at the time. As the taxi pulled up outside the store, a throng of people crowded around the taxi, staring in through the windows at my wife, not in any way aggressive or threatening, just very curious. I asked my wife to open the door to alight the taxi, but she hesitated, and I had to assure her that there was no danger at all, these people were just incredibly inquisitive. As she opened the door the throng literally parted, as if by magic, and the way was made clear for us to enter the store. Christine told me afterwards that although slightly scared, she realised that the people were of a very gentle nature and she didn't actually feel at all threatened, just a little intimidated and somewhat amazed and feeling a little like royalty!

We had a couple of good shopping expeditions in the store where prices were in two categories – one for the locals and the other, a much cheaper version, for the foreign visitors. One of our still prized possessions is a beautiful Chinese hearth rug, purchased in the store for £8. In 1971, when we carpeted our lounge in our first house in Cowes, I was offered £75 for that same rug by the carpet fitter who came to fit our new carpet! NO SALE! We still treasure that rug to this day, and although the tassels around each end of the rug are now looking a bit tatty, the main part of the intricately made and robust rug is still as good as it was when we bought it 53 years ago. Other purchases ranged from handkerchiefs and Hings underwear for me, a piece of faux fur for Christine to make herself a gilet with when we returned home and many other things that served us well for years.

The ships' agent in Shanghai was very taken that we had a young white woman on board, and arranged to take Christine to a state ballet performance one evening, which was being performed at the People's Palace Theatre in Shanghai while the ship was there. Christine, being an avid dance fan, immediately accepted the invitation, and was treated again a bit like royalty when she arrived at the theatre. Afterwards I asked her what the performance was like, and she revelled in its grace and beauty, but also commented that it was heavily politicised and told the story of the Great March of The People's Revolutionary Army with a lot of obvious propaganda contained within it. Nevertheless, quite an experience for a young English woman, and another notable memory from our trip together.

During that era of serving in the Merchant Navy, there was a lot of manual work that had to be done on the ships in connection with the cargo that we carried and the maintenance of the ship. One of these activities was the cleaning of the hatches after discharge and prior to loading the homeward-bound cargoes. This huge activity was too much for the ships' crews to undertake, and outside contractors would be assigned this job, usually in Japan where the ship would be mainly empty having discharged all her cargoes for Far Eastern ports and starting to reload for the European ports. Associated with this would of course be the 'backhanders', colloquially known as 'cumshaw', offered by different shore-based contractors vying for this lucrative work, and Chief Officers and Captains of ships could profit substantially from these unofficial payments – little brown envelopes flying back and forth! I watched it happening on most ships that I served on, but on the *Flintshire* our Chief Officer, Dai Jones, was one who did not accept any of these little 'sweeteners' for fear that any job quality that followed would not be of the highest standard – corners would be cut and there was no redress available after the event.

However, Dai did relent on this principle on one occasion to our benefit. The hatch cleaning supremo in Yokohama was one Yoshiyama, a respected citizen of the city who ran several lucrative businesses, one of which was providing hatch cleaning and dunnage refurbishment. Dunnage is low grade timber that is used to put under cases of cargo when they are stowed on steel decks in the hatches. It prevents 'sweating' and subsequent damage to the contents of the cases of cargo, and had to be renewed or cleaned regularly. Yoshiyama was no fool and made a lot of money out of these shipboard activities. He also owned several night clubs in and around Yokohama, and always offered a grand night out to the Chief Officers that he came into contact with. Dai would always refuse this perk, but on that trip when I had Christine with me, he relented and asked Yoshiyama if he would take the two of us ashore instead of himself. Yoshiyama readily agreed, and we were thus wafted into the main town of Yokohama like royalty in one of the biggest Japanese saloon cars I had ever seen. We entered one of his many night clubs and were entertained to a very pleasant evening out, with Christine being educated into the ways of Japanese culture. We both smoked at that time, and she was somewhat surprised that the hostesses in the club lit my cigarette first before hers – as is well known, gentlemen always come first in Japan.

Towards the end of the evening, Yoshiyama sidled up to Christine full of apologies and explained that as part of the entertainment a young lady would shortly appear on stage and, "Very Sorry, but tonight lady take off clothes." Amused, Christine assured him that she would not be embarrassed at all and thanked him for his concern. The lady did indeed 'take off clothes', but not all of them and the act was rather a modest and discreet performance. We returned to the ship in the wee small hours after an evening of dancing, drinking and being thoroughly well entertained.

The voyage did not go exactly as planned as later in that schedule I was asked to transfer to another outward-bound ship where the Second Officer had broken a bone in his foot in Hamburg immediately prior to sailing for Singapore, and there had not been time to arrange a relief for him from the UK. Whereas he could not entertain carrying out cargo operations with all the climbing up and down hatch ladders that it entailed, he could keep a bridge watch and assist in navigating the *Flintshire* home to the UK. I accepted the request on the provision that I could take Christine with me, and after a transfer by train from Penang to Port Swettenham, we joined the much newer *Glenfinlas* and set out to revisit the ports and sights of the Far East again. *Glenfinlas* was one of the eight 'Priam'- and 'Glenalmond'-class ships, with the redoubtable George Powell as Master, and Phil Harrison as the Chief Officer. Phil was a totally different kettle of fish to Dai Jones, accepting 'cumshaw' whenever and wherever it was offered.

The *Glenfinlas* was still outward bound on a slightly different schedule of ports to those of the *Flintshire* but on arrival back in Yokohama, Yoshiyama greeted Christine and me like long lost friends! There were other wives already aboard the *Glenfinlas* accompanying their respective husbands, and so with all these people in tow, Yoshiyama organised a minibus to take us all out for another night of revelry in Yokohama. We ate an early evening snack in a Yakatori House, and then went on to dance and be entertained in another of his clubs, named 'The Seventh Heaven', which was situated on the top floor of a department store, yet another one of Yoshiyama's enterprises!

Memories of that evening abound, there was a flute player in the group that was performing who could make his instrument 'talk' and one just had to get up and dance, such was his skill. The food was incredible, cold chicken cooked to perfection in a most amazing sauce and prawns that tasted like heaven. And of course, there was the almost inevitable stripper. She actually ended up sitting on our Radio Officer's lap, and when asked afterwards what it was like, Nibby said she was as cold as ice!

But the funniest thing to Christine and me about that evening in The Seventh Heaven was that Yoshiyama, ever the perfect Japanese gentleman, sidled up to Christine again and, full of apologies, announced to her discreetly that, "Very Sorry, but tonight lady take off ALL clothes!"

Flintshire.

Glenfinlas.

Cold Shivers Up and Down the Spine!

One of the major changes that affected all Pilots on the River Humber was the construction of the long-awaited Humber Bridge in the 1960s and '70s. This bridge had been promised for decades, and when it did eventually come, its construction was very welcome, joining the north and south banks of the river together and binding the two communities which had for so long been served by the ferries that operated from Hull to New Holland Pier. When finished it was, and still is, a spectacular sight that to this day draws visitors from all over the world who stand and marvel at its uncluttered simplicity and its sheer size. It was for some time the longest single span suspension bridge in the world, only to be surpassed a few years later by a bridge in Japan, incidentally built by the same builders who gave us our bridge across the Humber.

Navigating under it was equally spectacular, but there was always the prospect of an unplanned contact with the underside of it with a ship that was physically too tall to pass underneath the impressive centre span. The clearance under the bridge was always a bit of a mystery, and the father of a friend of my daughters, John Eden, was the Assistant Bridge Master. He was in effect the actual Bridge Master, as the Bridge Master designate was a local councillor who knew probably less about the bridge that he did about lamp posts. I did once ask John what the actual clearance was under the bridge, and he responded with a question as to what we, as Pilots, had actually been told. When I said that officially we had been told to allow 42.5 metres minus the height of tide on the gauge at Chalder Ness (the nearest tide gauge to the bridge itself) he just smiled, nodded and said, "Well I should continue using that!"

The magnificent Humber Suspension Bridge.
(Reproduced by kind permission of Pixabay.)

In the 1970s and '80s there were several large car carrying ships that plied their trade to Goole Docks, and they had what was termed a big 'air draft' – that is to say the distance from the water line of the ship to the tip of their signal/radar mast, which was usually mounted on their wheelhouse atop the structure of the ship. One of them was a German ship called the *Fredenhagen* and her air draft was in excess of the norm to pass under the bridge safely, so she had to be brought up to Hull Roads early in order that the Goole Pilot could take her under the bridge at a safe time on the rising tide, then turn the ship round to 'stem' the incoming tidal current in the deep water just above the bridge. There the ship could await the tide to rise some more before turning around once again to continue to Goole when there was sufficient depth of water for her to safely pass the shallows that existed further up the river. This understandably was inconvenient for all concerned, and the owners of the ship had arranged to have the upper bit of this signal mast cut off during an upcoming routine dry docking and thus reduce her air draft.

On her very last trip before this scheduled dry docking, she arrived a little late and was brought up to Hull Roads post haste to be boarded by the Goole Pilot, and he hurried up towards the bridge. Whether he missed passing under the centre of the span where there was maximum clearance or he was indeed too late, the ship's upper topmast, the bit that was to be removed soon afterwards, clipped the underside of the bridge, and while doing no damage to the bridge structure, apart from scratching the paint, it ended up hanging at a crazy angle until a large crane was summoned in Goole and engineers removed the offending bit and landed it on the ship's deck. The Goole Pilot's damage report was never seen by anyone other than the authority, but we held bets as to its content and how he had explained away doing the dry dock's job for them.

Some months after that incident, I was waiting for a ship to come down from Goole to take over from the Goole Pilot, Greg David, and take the ship, the *Starman Anglia*, on the last leg of her long passage from Goole, that is from Hull Roads to sea. She was expected at about 0700, and I was patiently awaiting her arrival in the Pilot Office in Hull, having been summoned earlier that day to attend at the office for the only 'Goole ebb'. The *Starman Anglia* was a specialised heavy lift ship which could undertake many differing roles, being able to accept heavy lifts up to 300 tons with her massive Stülcken derrick, or accept 'roll on/roll off' cargoes from a dock side via her stern ramp. She was extremely versatile, being specially built and strengthened to additionally sit on the bottom without a drop of water around her at all and load cargoes over her stern, again via her stern ramp, which was designed to reach any surface she was sitting on. A true hybrid design built in 1977 with innovative British engineering design and skills on the River Tyne by Swan Hunters, she served for nearly 30 years before being broken up by her third owners in 2006.

She had arrived in Goole a few days earlier carrying a large unwieldly heavy lift on her deck, to which the lifting hook of her massive Stülcken derrick was still attached to provide the load with some more security whilst the ship was on passage at sea. After she had discharged her load to heavy lift road transporters in Goole Docks, her crew had restowed the derrick in its more normal upright position before the ship left the docks for her passage to sea.

Greg David, the Pilot, had successfully negotiated the trickier part of the trip downriver towards Hull, and after eating his breakfast that had been brought to the wheelhouse by the ship's steward, and it being a beautiful spring morning, he decided to take some air outside the wheelhouse while the ship was on a relatively straight leg of the bendy passage that was the norm 'upriver'. Watching the sun rise behind the South Tower of the Humber Bridge, he suddenly suffered a bout of 'cold shivers' up and down his spine. Turning around to look at the neatly stowed vertical mass of the Stülcken derrick way up in the air, he dashed back into the wheelhouse and demanded to know from the officer of the watch, "What the hell is your air draft?" Meeting surprised and stunned looks on the face of the Watch Officer and the Master of the ship, he simply pointed towards the rapidly approaching bridge wondering whether he was going to make a name for himself as a bridge wrecker!

When the ship had gone up to Goole, her derrick had been lowered with the lifting hook attached to the cargo she was carrying, thus making it much lower. Now, with the derrick neatly stowed in its more normal position, flying proudly vertical, it threatened to hit the bridge extremely hard and probably do much damage as a result. The crew of the ship were quickly turned out of their bunks, and Greg turned the ship round to 'stem' the outpouring and falling tide. The process of lowering the derrick from its vertical stance to a height where the ship could safely pass under the bridge was carried out as quickly as possible, but it still took some time to remove the safety lashings that held it there, and all the time Greg was concerned that the tide was falling away rapidly and that he may not have enough water underneath the ship to reach Hull Roads once past the bridge.

He did just make it through without running aground and survived what could have been a very nasty accident with severe repercussions. As Greg said afterwards, "Thank God I just took that short stroll out on to the bridge wing to take the air and watch the sun rising behind the magnificent bridge tower, otherwise there would have been one almighty bang!" Those 'shivers up and down his spine' certainly saved the day.

Sitting in the office waiting for the ship to arrive in the Roads, I was completely oblivious to all this – the only message I had received from the operator in Hull Radio was that there was a bit of a problem and the ship would be a little later than previously predicted. All the details of this tale were related to me by the slightly rattled Master of the ship after I had eventually boarded her and was on passage to sea.

When I saw Greg some days after the incident, he went on to say that he didn't know how he had managed to negotiate the National Grid electricity power cables that were strung across the River Ouse at Yokefleet. All he could think of was that he had stuck closer to the river bank at that point, and not passed under the centre of the span of those cables and the lowest part of the catenary – if he'd brought those down it would have blacked out half of Yorkshire.

It wasn't until some years later that the Lower Station Humber Pilots were amalgamated with the Goole and Trent Pilots and we started to experience some of the worries that they had previously coped with, and that we Lower Station men in our ignorance had dismissed as irrelevant. It certainly added to the complications of the job as a whole and made us more appreciative of what the upriver Pilots had experienced for all those years!

Lapad, formerly the *Starman Anglia* – derrick down.
Photo courtesy of Patrick Hill.

Starman Anglia – derrick up.
Photo courtesy of Michael Green.

Nettle Wine and 'Specials'

There were many characters in SeaSpeed, not only among the flight crew but in the office and general staff and also among the engineering section. One of the engineers was a likeable, amiable chap called Danny Chalk, a local Isle of Wight man whose father had set up and ran a successful heavy plant hire company on the island. Politely declining his father's offer of a comfortable job within the company, Danny set out to be as independent as he could be and joined British Rail Engineering to carve out a career of his own.

Many of the engineers who worked in SeaSpeed were initially trained by British Rail Engineering for maintaining gas turbines, as they were originally designated to be fitted to the high-speed trains that were developed in the late-1960s and early '70s and finally introduced in 1975. The Intercity 125 trains were eventually fitted with high-speed diesels and not gas turbines, but the expertise was there to be tapped, and many of the engineers arrived in SeaSpeed via this route as the natural choice to look after the hovercraft power plants which were Rolls Royce gas turbines of differing genres.

Danny came to SeaSpeed this way and, being an islander originally, started to set himself up resident back on the Isle of Wight. He was very popular with his colleagues in the Engineering Department, with the Hovercraft Commanders and the terminal staff, and not being married, he always volunteered for those slightly unusual late-night jobs that occasionally cropped up. He bought a brand new house on the outskirts of Newport (the island's 'capital') and typical of the new builds of that era, his garden was a muddy wasteland, completely covered in tall nettles. Not being a wasteful sort, Danny harvested all the nettles and proceeded to turn them into wine, making about 20 gallons of the stuff that was stored in demi-johns in his attic. Being the sociable type, Danny would always invite the Commanders of any late-night specials to his house for a night cap once they had parked the craft and were finished for the night. I remember going to Danny's house one night with Ken Blackwood shortly after this concoction had been produced and was offered a glass of Danny's nettle wine. To say it was horrible would be an understatement; it was totally awful, unpalatable and undrinkable! And Danny had manufactured 20 gallons of the stuff!

Not one to throw anything away, Danny simply said that he would keep it and hope it would improve with age. I'm afraid that both Ken and I were of the opinion that this was wishful thinking but, accepting a cold beer from Danny, we whiled away an hour or so chatting before proceeding home to our respective houses.

During my first season with SeaSpeed, working the Portsmouth to Ryde route with the HM2 sidewall hovercraft, one of our regulars was the late Cliff Michelmore, a popular television and radio presenter of the time. Having been born on the Isle of Wight, he had a home on the island as well as a flat in London near Broadcasting House which he shared with his wife Jean Metcalfe, another famous broadcaster of the day. He would always ask if he could come onto the flight deck for the 10-minute crossing from Portsmouth, and we got to know and like him as he was always chatty and a diversion from the daily duty of driving that particular machine. He used the Portsmouth to Ryde route as his home was close to one of the stations on the island's railway line that operated from Ryde Pier Head to Sandown and Shanklin. He would travel from London to Portsmouth on the train, walk the short distance to the hovercraft terminal at the end of the station pier at Portsmouth, cross with us to Ryde, and then board a train at Ryde Pier Head station to his home without having to walk very far between 'links', particularly convenient after a busy, tiring day programme making.

Cliff was also a popular figure with a lot of the other stars of the day, and in particular with the late Dickie Henderson, a wonderful all-round entertainer whom Cliff and his wife Jean made personal friends with. When Cliff had Dickie Henderson in tow, the pair of them would crowd into the flight deck with us and Dickie would keep us amused and entertained while we crossed the Solent. Dickie was also a bit scatter-brained, professional to a tee when on stage, but an abysmal organiser of his professional life and the dates he promised to fulfil in his hard-working schedule. He was also an avid charity worker – he gave free concerts and gigs all over the place whilst undertaking paid work and would squeeze these extra dates in wherever he could. One memorable occasion was when he was staying on the island with Cliff Michelmore, he managed to virtually double book himself. He made a promise to do a charity event at Bournemouth Pier Theatre while appearing twice nightly at a theatre in Sandown. He was of course staying with Cliff Michelmore at his home, Dickie being a hater of hotels that he had to stay in when touring, so the offer of home life at the Michelmores was gratefully accepted.

Now, there was a serious problem. Sandown is on the south-eastern side of the Isle of Wight, and Bournemouth Pier is on the mainland, some 30 miles away along a stretch of English Channel. Resourceful to the end, Cliff Michelmore approached us to see if we could help. As I would be the duty 'Standby Man' on the day in question, I was contacted by the Route Manager of the day, a very go-ahead replacement for the previous Route Manager who had been promoted to the Head Office of British Rail in London to slow things down there! I worked out that with a full tank of fuel (220 gallons) on the craft we could make it back to Cowes at the end of the trip with about 50 gallons left, the minimum reserve that was required by the rules and regulations laid down by the Civil Aviation Authority. We did also have 100 gallons spare in the ballast tanks (that were used to trim the craft during flight) but these reserves were never used as they sat in those tanks ad infinitum and the quality of that fuel was doubtful to say the least! We would also require from the Civil Aviation Authority a special dispensation to travel outside our normal operating area, which was chased up immediately by our new enthusiastic and 'go-ahead' Route Manager. A second man to navigate would also be needed as it was almost a completely 'dark' flight and radar would be required, so John Summers was contacted and he agreed to come in and navigate for me.

Dispensations being obtained on the proviso that we carried a Flight Engineer as well, all was set, Danny Chalk readily volunteering for this latter role. We departed the Cowes hovercraft terminal at 2030 with fuel tanks full to busting, and proceeded 'North about' around the island through the Solent to cover the 15 miles and land on the beach at Sandown alongside the pier. Dickie Henderson finished his 8 o'clock show at about 2130 and, with Cliff Michelmore in tow, boarded the craft and we set off along the south coast of the island towards Bournemouth. I had previously travelled to Bournemouth to liaise with the local Town Council, to seek permission to land on the beach alongside the pier, and to 'suss out' the local area and possible access points on the pier itself. Armed with all this information and the permission to proceed, we were blessed with an almost perfect night for flying. There was a light south-westerly wind, visibility was excellent, no swell at all and with John installed on the radar and passenger cabin lights out so as not to distract me from flying and John from navigating, we shot off to cover the 32 miles from Sandown to Bournemouth. We achieved this in a little under 40 minutes, arriving on the beach alongside the pier at about 2225.

Dickie was just about in time for his appearance on stage, where he was scheduled to perform as the star turn for about 40 minutes at an event to raise money in the early days of the Cancer Research Charity. We were all invited to attend the event on the pier, but the craft had to be kept manned at all times, so John Summers and Danny went up to the theatre and enjoyed what they said afterwards was a memorable performance. Typical of Dickie Henderson, he overran his time being totally oblivious of the clock and appeared again after about an hour on stage. He was due to re-appear for the second show of the night at Sandown at midnight, but after re-boarding the craft on the beach at the pier around 2345, there was no way we could get him back in time for his scheduled appearance. Using the VHF radio on the craft, I called the operator at Niton Radio, the local Isle of Wight coast radio station, explained our predicament and, bless him, amidst all his current duties and being a fan of Dickie Henderson, he rang the theatre at Sandown to explain that we would be a little late, but were en route! In fact, we landed back at Sandown about 0020, and Dickie appeared back on stage to rapturous applause at about 0030 – half an hour late but still full of energy after his long evening out at work.

It was one of those unusual tasks that we were very occasionally asked to fulfil, and it was very enjoyable if a little challenging being out of our normal comfortable work area that we knew so well. The icing on the cake was of course that after we returned to Cowes and landed, re-fuelled the craft to replenish the now slightly empty tanks, washed the engine and shut the craft down, Danny, the ever-hospitable socialite invited us back to his house for a night cap. John and I looked at each other – could this mean another stab at the awful nettle wine? Neither of us had been to his house for a while, but we accepted, knowing that beers would be available if the wine was still undrinkable!

The 'stretched' BHC SR.N6 Mark 1 S. During type conversion training for Commanders, shortly after delivery to SeaSpeed, being flown by Commander Jeremy Walker with Commander John Bishop observing.

We had absolutely no problems at all though. The wine had matured over the three-year gap since we had first tasted it, and it was as smooth, tasty and full bodied as could be. Other Commanders had sampled the wine through the intervening period and had commented that it was improving, but was still not a classic! However, on that night John and I sampled it to the full and I don't actually remember driving home to Cowes and dropping John off at his home on the way, so that wine certainly made its mark!

And so, to Pastures New – Part 1

In January of 2002, after a long and drawn-out dispute with the Port Authority on the Humber, I, along with all my other 120 Humber Pilot colleagues, had my authorisation – the modern equivalent of a Pilot's Licence – revoked by the authority and my right to work on the River Humber was taken away from me. After 27 years of devoted service to the Estuary, the Humber Pilot Service, of which I had been a very proud member, and its customers, I felt the blow very hard, and I could not work for some 18 months after that sad event. However, I felt that I was not 'done' yet and did not want to 'hang up my boots'.

The Humber Pilots have a very active website, and a message appeared one day on the site that the Chief Officer of the *Waverley* was seeking a relief for her leave period. So it was that a couple of weeks later I travelled to Birkenhead to join the *Waverley* where she was sitting in dry dock. *Waverley* is the last steam-powered, ocean-going, passenger carrying paddle steamer in the world and was a magnificent site to behold when travelling at speed through the calm waters of the Clyde where she was based. She had encountered a bit of a problem and had struck the bottom off Sanda Island whilst on a cruise around the Mull of Kintyre and ended up with some bottom damage, hence her sojourn in the dry dock.

After settling in on board we left the dry dock and sailed down the Mersey, bringing back to me poignant memories of many years previously when I had served in Blue Funnel Line's ships, and Liverpool was their home port. We sailed back to the Clyde to resume the ship's set of scheduled services, travelling up and down the Clyde taking Glaswegians 'doon the watter'. There were many people I met whilst there, and among the more notable were Timothy West and Prunella Scales, who joined the ship for a short hop from Greenock to Dunoon to reacquaint themselves with their favourite ship. They were 'friends' of the *Waverley*, and as well as chartering her for their wedding anniversary party on the Thames some years before, they supported the trust that owns and runs the ship, and take an active interest in her.

There were many cruises that we did on the Clyde, but the most enjoyable were the trips through the stunningly beautiful Kyles of Bute to Tighnabruaich. The Kyles is a particularly narrow channel with very little clearance on either side of the ship's paddle boxes, and on advice from the Master, I left it to the Helmsman on duty at the time to 'take her through'. Immediately after the rigours of passing through the Kyles is a large turn to port and, with the *Waverley* heeling over at an angle while travelling at speed in order to maintain a flow over the rudder and keep steerage way and control of her, this was quite a sight to see!

Arrival at Tighnabruaich Pier was impressive with an enterprising young local lad, who was no more than 12 or 13 years old, having installed himself on the pierhead playing his bagpipes to entertain the assembled passengers as we came alongside. After we had tied up there and the passengers had streamed off to take in the delights of the village, I went down on to the pier to ask this young entrepreneur how he had got on. The young piper pointed to his bagpipe case, conveniently left wide open at his feet on the quay, and it was apparent that he had done very well indeed! It was said afterwards that on a good day he could pick up 60 or 70 pounds in pocket money, and I have to say, he earned it!

Passing through the Kyles of Bute.

Whilst aboard the *Waverley* I learned some new and novel ship handling techniques, the likes of which I had never seen or tried before. The way of 'sweeping past' the berth on a sort of curved track, then putting the paddles into 'full astern' and popping her alongside 'backwards' was truly amazing to watch, and the Master, Captain Collard, did allow me to play once or twice – under close supervision of course! I spent a couple of happy weeks aboard, plying the Clyde and enjoying this totally new way of life, visiting some places I had never been before. It also brought back memories of holidays caravanning in Scotland with my family when we had toured many places around the lochs and glens of the west coast of that beautiful country. What amazed me about the *Waverley* was her very large turning circle, which was demonstrated to me in Loch Goil after cruising in there on a sightseeing cruise from Dunoon. The approach and turn had to be very carefully executed otherwise we would have ended up aground on one shore or other of the loch!

Because the paddles on any steam-powered paddle steamer are fixed together, simply attached to each end of the massive crank shaft of the huge horizontally mounted steam engine that drives the ship, they are not able to be 'split' with one paddle going one way and the other the opposite way, which would have made the ship very manoeuvrable and easy to handle. Some other diesel electric paddle powered ships and ferries were able to 'split' their paddles and turn in their own length, but not the dear old *Waverley*! Restricted as she was led to a rather exciting manoeuvre called 'canting', which we had to do to turn the ship around in the narrow confines of the River Clyde. This manoeuvre, which I had never seen before, was carried out after we had tied up and discharged passengers, and was the last act of the day before bedding her down for the night. A heavy and very strong rope was stretched from the bows the full length of the ship down the 'off side' – the side away from the quay which she was tied up to – taken around the stern and then made fast on the quay behind where she was laid. All the other ropes were then let go, and we steamed ahead very slowly on the engines, which caused the ship to swing around in a tight circle, restricted and held back by this 'canting rope' and thus, the ship ended up pointing the other way ready for the next day's outings.

But my everlasting memory of that two-week period was when, one night, whilst assisting nearly 500 Glaswegians to disembark at the quay in Glasgow, a large proportion of whom were somewhat 'worse for wear', I heard this almighty splash.

Glaswegians have an overwhelming desire to have fun and enjoy themselves. Boarding for the 'Trip Doon The Watter' they made a beeline for one of the many bars situated on board, and when these bars opened immediately after the ship had left Anderston Quay at 10am, many of them remained firmly installed beside the bar until we returned some 12 hours later back in Glasgow. Not for them the scenic beauty of the Firth of Clyde or the ports we visited – they just wanted to stay and take their pleasure in their own inimitable way! There were all sorts of diversions for the passengers to occupy themselves while we cruised down the River Clyde, then the Firth of Clyde and the Kyles of Bute to Tighnabruaich, calling at several ports en route to take on and discharge passengers who chose to do segments of the cruise rather than spend the whole day aboard. There was also plenty of entertainment provided on board for the assembled throngs, with restaurants and fast food readily available, cooked by our long-suffering catering staff who worked incredibly hard and for very long hours.

'Canting' the *Waverley* at Victoria Pier, Goole. The 'canting rope' can be seen stretching across the photograph from the ship's bows on the right, across the paddle box, and to the quay at the left of the photograph. (Photo courtesy of the late Goole Pilot, Peter Blud.)

Music was abundant, and one band was a truly traditional Scottish country dance music band with accordions, fiddles, guitars and drums, but thankfully no bagpipes – that was reserved for the young lad at Tighnabruaich! They played requests for the gathered throng, as well as their own repertoire. Scottish country dance music is not a favourite of mine, but it went down very well and helped the passengers enjoy their day out. One tune had been written by a member of the band celebrating the *Waverley* and her trips 'doon the watter' and was played repeatedly. However, after almost 12 hours of near non-stop music and the relentless repeating of that one tune – it did sometimes wear a little thin!

Thus, it was when in the middle of offloading our guests at the quay on our return at 2130 that I heard this commotion from the other side of the ship. Alerted by the alarmed cries from other passengers I rushed to the side of the ship away from the quay, to observe one rather inebriated gentleman wallowing around in the shallow waters of the Clyde! He had obviously decided that he wasn't going to join the long queue of people waiting to leave the ship by one of the three gangways to the quay, and so he tried the other side, calmly walking off the ship and falling into the river. In fact, the water was so shallow that he was standing on the bottom uttering profanities and looking rather cross! Being in charge, I had no option but to very quickly disrobe as far as decency permitted, clamber down to the lowest part of the paddle box and jump off the ship myself into the rather chilly waters of the River Clyde to assist in getting him back aboard. The other crew members were there to assist of course, but I was very glad that it was summertime and not later in the year when the *Waverley* would still have been running in much cooler water!

I did two weeks aboard as Chief Officer, and at the end of it the Master, Captain Collard, who was the Senior Captain in the company at the time, asked me if I would stay on board for a couple of extra days in a consultancy capacity to compile a report on the grounding that the ship had suffered, and make recommendations. This was my first taste of consultancy outside my days as a Pilot, and the report I made was accepted and acted upon, which was very gratifying.

The Chief Officer had asked me to return to relieve her again a few weeks later so she could take some more leave, but circumstances changed very quickly in those rather heady days post piloting, and another former Humber Pilot colleague, Alastair Reed, contacted me and asked if I would be prepared to take on something a little different.

Since the demise of the Pilot Service on the Humber, he had been operating a ferry in the Shetland Islands, based on the incredibly remote island of Foula. One of the lesser known and more distant islands in the group way to the north of the mainland of the British Isles, Foula is situated 15 miles to the west of the mainland of Shetland itself, stuck out in the remoteness of the mighty Atlantic Ocean. Much is talked about another Shetland Island, Fair Isle, which itself is remotely situated part way between the Shetland mainland and the archipelago of the Orkney Islands, and it is subject to some pretty foul weather. But Foula is even more exposed to rough weather and storms, with nothing to the west of it but the Atlantic, and the next stop is America. Alastair had warned me of the rigours of taking on such a task, but I eagerly agreed to give it a go, and travelled some days later, flying to Aberdeen and then taking a flight to Sumburgh on Shetland. On arrival at Sumburgh, the dreaded fog had descended on the airport making it impossible, even after three attempts, for the aircraft to land, and the 'duck out' airport for Shetland is... Aberdeen!

On returning to Aberdeen we had been booked by the airline on the overnight Northlink ferry to Lerwick, and after a mad scramble from the airport to the port of Aberdeen by taxi, I boarded the ferry for the trip to Shetland...

And so, to Pastures New – Part 2

Approaching Shetland for the first time, I viewed the vista from the deck of the Northlink ferry as we approached and was immediately taken by the scene that unfolded before me. Never having been north of John o' Groats before, the view was one of peace and tranquillity, something that I was to learn more intimately when I took up my new position as Master of the Foula ferry. After travelling by taxi from Lerwick to Walls, the small haven on the west coast of the mainland of Shetland where the ferry terminal was situated, I waited for the *New Advance* to arrive from Foula and took in the calm atmosphere that pervades everywhere in Shetland. No hustle and bustle here, just water, water everywhere and hardly any traffic at all, either on land or sea.

Eventually my new 'charge' came into view, passing through the narrow channels that marked the entrance to the 'voe' – the local name for the small inlets that were everywhere within the Shetland chain of islands. Alastair Reed, my former Humber Pilot colleague who I was relieving, had warned me that she wasn't very big, but my first look at her still took me by surprise! A mere 38 feet in length powered by two big diesels, she had an ungainly top-heavy look about her with a large structure on her foredeck and a low aspect towards her stern. Watching her come alongside with her small crew dashing about to make her fast filled me with confidence – these were islanders who knew what they were doing!

Ever the optimist, I boarded to be greeted by Alastair, who I had not seen for 18 months since January 2002 when we did our last day on the Humber as Pilots. The handover was somewhat, of necessity, rather brief as Alastair was booked on a flight to take him home to England, and then a flight to New Zealand for a much-needed holiday. I was introduced to the rest of the crew, Keith the Chief Officer, Steve the Engineer, and a crew 'man' who I mistook for a fellow but who was in fact one of the crofters on the island with a part-time job as a deck hand on the ferry – and *she* was called Annie! So, with my crew of four in total, we departed a couple of hours later to sail to Foula. Departing the voe at Walls was somewhat tricky as I'd never even seen it before, but a very clever chart plotter coupled to a satellite navigator got me out of it without incident, the courses having been preloaded into the chart plotter and laid out clearly before me on an easy-to-read screen.

The *New Advance.*

My first sight of Foula, with its five distinctive peaks in the distance some 15 miles away to the west, filled me with some excitement, and the prospect of living there for three weeks and operating this small but obviously very capable ferry filled me with some exhilaration, despite the slightly daunting challenge to my skills and expertise. The first crossing went without incident in calm weather – just the ever-present Atlantic swell gently providing some motion to the boat on the passage. I got a chance to acquaint myself with my new crew during the crossing and, arriving two hours later at Ham Voe, the tiny inlet on the east coast of Foula where we were to berth and stay, I asked Keith, the Chief Officer who was an islander, to take her in and allow me to watch and learn. I think I endeared myself to my crew for that act, as they were as unsure of me as I was of them, and respect is earned, not a right to be expected. We started to unload as soon as we arrived, and then came the unusual act of lifting her out of the water into her cradle on the quayside, something that was totally new to me with something so large and heavy. The weather in Foula can change incredibly quickly and turn extremely violent, endangering the ferry's safety if left afloat, so to avoid this she was hoisted on two massive davits clean out of the water every night. This left me somewhat in awe of the massive engineering that had been installed to carry out this operation, and apart from manoeuvring the ferry into position, I left the crew and the engineer to do the nitty gritty.

Keith, the Chief Officer, and his wife Margot ran the bed and breakfast on the island for visitors, and this is where the ferry operators, the Shetland Islands Council, had a permanent booking for the visiting Masters of the ferry. Settling in to my new temporary home, I was made very welcome, but detected an atmosphere between the two hosts. Later on in my tenure, I discovered that these two hosts were a little 'estranged' and Keith had been thrown out of the B & B to live in a converted, rather ramshackle cottage adjacent to the house. This was confirmed later by the news that when a radio programme had been made about the residents of the island, Keith and Margot had been referred to as the Basil and Sybil Fawlty of the Shetlands! I managed however to merge into the scenario and got down to the business of taking the ferry bookings, generally looking after the running of the system and of course 'driving' my new charge.

Lifting her out of the water.

Stowed and snug in her cradle.

We only ran three days a week, carrying everything that the islanders needed that the aeroplane service that also operated couldn't carry, mainly the heavier items such as the livestock that was prevalent on Foula, cars, fuel for the diesel generators that provided the electricity (from 0700 to midnight every day!) and the road stone that was sent across in one-ton bags for repairing the island's roads. Everyone on the island had at least two jobs. Keith maintained the roads, looked after the lighthouse at the south end of the island and was of course the Chief Officer on the ferry. Steve the engineer looked after all the ferry's needs and the equipment on the quayside in Ham Voe that serviced the boat and lifted her out of the water every night. Annie was, what seemed to me, the only hard-working crofter left on the island; she worked very hard cultivating the meagre land and rearing animals, pigs, sheep, and a very few cattle which she milked for the populace.

The man who was regarded as the 'Laird' was a statuesque man called Jim Gaunt who, together with his son and daughter-in-law, John and Sarah, claimed the ownership of the herd of Shetland ponies on the island as well as most of the 5,000 sheep that roamed freely. John Gaunt also had a job on the ferry as relief Chief Officer, and his wife Sarah also helped out at the school. Jim Gaunt also ran the electricity supply along with Steve the engineer who maintained the diesels situated in a building next to the Community Hall and the primary school.

Altogether a busy little community of only 30 people in total, who I had romantically expected to be a hard-working bunch of crofters and fishermen striving to eke out a living from the land and surrounding sea, but who in fact seemed to sit back and wait for the many available subsidies that came apparently with ease from the Shetland Island and Highland and Island Councils. The money from these grants was, however, vital to ensure the continuance of the community, and they all helped each other out when necessary by assisting in some of the activities that went on, as well as assisting when misfortune occurred. A house fire caused by one of the elderly inhabitants lighting his stove using a diesel-soaked rag that went somewhat wrong was dealt with immediately by the other residents, and he was accommodated while his house was repaired and rebuilt.

I settled in to the ways of the island quickly, probably because I was not a stranger to 'island life', having previously lived on the Isle of Wight, but there was no real comparison. There were no shops on the island at all apart from the Post Office, manned by Sarah Gaunt, Jim's wife, and that only sold postcards and stamps. Everything that was consumed on the island was carried by the ferry or the aeroplane that ran four times a week on a single daily flight from Tingwall on the mainland. The plane of course could only carry a limited amount of food if the ferry wasn't running due to the weather, so we carried everything else. Fuel for the many rickety cars that were on the island was transported in five-gallon jerry cans on deck, as were the two 3-ton fuel bowsers that were on trailers and portable so that they could be brought and stowed in the hatch below decks of the ferry for refilling from a road tanker at Walls. We had a capacity to carry 12 passengers as well, although we were never full of passengers, and we also carried cars from the mainland to the island when someone bought a 'new one', to use a very casual description! They were all MOT car test failures, didn't need any tax or insurance, and were just run until they worked no longer and then abandoned wherever they 'died'.

These cars were kept unlocked and always had their keys in them – if you needed to get from one end of the island to the other quickly for any reason, you simply took a car and left it wherever you wanted to be – someone would always need it for a reverse journey and the system simply worked without any formality!

Carriage of the ponies and sheep for market was one of the main exports of the island, and as the ponies on Foula were the last remaining pure breed of Shetlands left, they commanded a high price on the open market. Seemingly all the other islands within the group had allowed their ponies to be interbred with other strains of pony from outside the Shetlands, and these highly prized Foula ponies were much in demand. They were lovely, docile little animals that were not afraid of humans at all, and one could approach them and stroke them without any fear whatsoever.

I did arrange for my wife to join me from home in East Yorkshire for a week during one of my periods of duty whilst I was on Foula, and we went out for a full day's walking around the three mile by two mile island. Stopping for our packed lunch high above the sea on the side of one of the five peaks that dominated the skyline of the island, we were suddenly aware that we were not alone. One of the ponies that roamed the countryside freely had seen us and decided to investigate. After eating our sandwiches, we had rounded them off with my personal version of 'Scottish' chocolate liqueurs, which consisted of a piece of chocolate washed down with a swig of neat Scotch from my hip flask, and were eating our bags of crisps, to be disturbed by a sweet little pony nuzzling into my wife's crisp bag and helping himself! Totally unfazed by these two insurgents, he had decided that he was peckish and simply joined us.

Lunch with the locals!

There were so many fascinating characters among the locals, even in such a small tight-knit community, and I was in awe at some of the stories that were told. Ernest Ballantine was one of the oldest of the residents who revelled in traditional folk music, and even though he was not connected to the island's electricity system, being resident at the south end of the island, he had installed solar and wind power for his battery system into his isolated cottage so that he could listen to his enormous collection of CDs and records. I was told that one very famous American folk singer had visited Ernie and spent the whole stay just playing his guitar along with Ernie, and had marvelled at the knowledge that Ernie had of the music world outside the confines of the island. Indeed, the ordinary world outside held no attraction whatsoever for Ernie, and he had only been off the island twice in his whole long life. He apparently travelled to Scalloway on the mainland for a holiday but left after a week as he said there were too many bodies and not enough room to walk freely. The only other time he had been to the mainland was when he was evacuated by helicopter following a heart attack, and even then, he couldn't wait to get back to his home tucked away in the peaceful and quiet corner of his beloved island.

I visited him on a couple of occasions to have a chat and see how he was, and at the same time I took the opportunity to take a walk to the south end of the island to see the lighthouse. The second time I went, there was a very strong gale blowing, and I ventured to walk out to the shore, curious to observe the conditions. I am no fairy in stature, quite the reverse in fact, but the wind was so strong that at one point it actually blew me off my feet, and while on the ground I could feel the spray that was being thrown up from the huge waves that, after having crashed into the 200-foot-high cliffs and careering skywards, was then whipped across the land by the incredibly strong wind. Quite a sight and one I will never forget.

We did carry many different cargoes during my sojourn there, many for supporting the general life of the islanders, but also some interesting ones too. We mainly ran between Ham Voe and Walls, but on one occasion every fortnight, our Thursday sailing was to Scalloway so that any of the locals could commute to Lerwick easily and access the shops and facilities there. Walls was rather poorly served by the Shetland transport system, being only a small outpost of the mainland community, but Scalloway had a regular and quick bus service that made it easy to get to Lerwick. But our main and most regular call was at Walls, where we discharged the island's exports of livestock. It was also the place where we loaded the wrecks of cars purchased by the residents bound for the island, and any unusual shipments of all kinds of odd items.

On one occasion we had Annie as a casual passenger for the trip to Walls. On arrival we observed this Land Rover with a medium-sized brand-new livestock trailer hitched to the back of it. Annie keenly dashed ashore after we had berthed to examine its contents, and when I had the chance I also went ashore to view the trailer and work out how we were going to load it on board. Opening the doors at the rear, I was amazed to see four delightful little rare breed piglets that Annie had decided to add to her livestock collection, and over the three months that I served on the island, I watched them grow into feisty little additions to the life of the island! They were real little characters in their own right and seemed to fit into the general atmosphere of eccentricity with ease. They used to escape occasionally, and the islanders would all congregate and search to shepherd them back into their rightful home with Annie at her croft.

Food for the residents was one of the main necessities to be carried. For this we had a large, what I can only describe as a stainless steel portable 'cupboard' that we had carried empty from Foula, and which was then filled with the cartons of food ordered over the phone by the residents, delivered to the jetty at Walls or Scalloway by the local supermarket's delivery drivers. Coal, bricks for house repairs, even a small JCB digger perched precariously on deck were all shipped to the island, providing of course the weather played ball. There were many occasions when we had to cancel the service due to the conditions, but we simply tried to defer the sailings to a day with better weather, and it just worked – the islanders were true pragmatists who accepted what life threw at them without complaint – well not too much anyway!

My recollections of life there are filled with great admiration of the people I met, and with the dialect that I tried (and failed!) to master. I had a telephone call one day from one of the other residents, a lady called Mary of very advanced years who managed her own small flock of sheep and sold her sheep and lambs to the mainland on a regular basis. Having a conversation with her really needed an interpreter, as her brogue and way of talking was very broad 'Foula'. I remember the first of these conversations vividly when she asked me if I could take "Farty beasts and thirty fower yow lamsch" to the mainland for market. What, I thought, was a 'yow lamsch' and how many was 'farty'? Hastily getting hold of Keith, I queried this request, and he simply translated it to "Forty beasts and thirty-four ewe lambs", and all became clear! We took them the following day, Mary having driven them all on her own to the quayside for loading and then disappearing back to her house and croft to carry on nurturing her flocks.

'Yow lamschs' for shipment.

Ponies for the mainland.

Carrying the animals across that stormy stretch of waters to the mainland and destinations unknown to us did not seem to faze the stock at all, and we must have shipped a couple of hundred or so animals across the seas in my short time working there. The lambs were from a particularly hardy breed and were used for breeding purposes all over the United Kingdom, their stamina and weather resistance being widely accredited and well renowned.

But my time in Shetland was to come to a slightly premature end as I had a surprise phone call one evening while still resident at the B & B on Foula from another former Humber Pilot colleague, Dave Evans, who had actually left the service in 2001 to go and work in another pilotage district, that of Peterhead in Scotland. He asked me if I was prepared to go and work in Peterhead as a Pilot for a short-term, temporary, 12-week contract to cover for him and his other colleagues while he went away for a long-planned holiday to America. The Senior Pilot in Peterhead was sadly very ill, and the other two Pilots, of whom Dave was one, could not cover the roster alone without some additional manpower. The prospect of true piloting once again was too much for me to resist, and I hastily and very readily agreed. While I was home on leave from that last tour of duty in Shetland, I had a telephone interview with the Harbour Master, and was accepted to start immediately.

My final trip 'in command' of the *New Advance* was in early October and, having taken the booking for two skips of island rubbish to be shipped to Walls the next day, destined to be burnt in Lerwick's incinerator to help heat the local hospital and old folks' homes, I took my last walk up Hamnafield on the day before that last trip. Looking down at Foula from on high and taking in that unforgettable view of my 'massive' ferry stowed in her cradle on the quayside over 1,000 feet below me, I wondered how, after my moderately successful career at sea of 42 years so far, I had ended up driving a floating dust cart!

My floating dust cart, complete with two skips of rubbish aboard.

Where on earth, I wondered, would I end up next ...?

PRINTED AND BOUND BY:
Copytech (UK) Limited trading as Printondemand-worldwide,
9 Culley Court, Bakewell Road, Orton Southgate.
Peterborough, PE2 6XD, United Kingdom.